Reflecti

"**I wish there wasn't a need to write this book. But there is.** Too often, we forget that being a mature follower of Jesus does not require that we be married. As April so eloquently describes through stories from her life and scripture, singleness is not second best to marriage. Single life can be complete life. Single life can be full life. And single life can be the Jesus life. **If you have ever wrestled with singleness, either your own or someone else's, read this book.**"

   - Mark Wessner, President
   Mennonite Brethren Seminary

"Throughout my years of walking in singleness, I have never read a book like *And If I Don't?* that gives so much hope, resonates so deeply with my heart struggles, and offers such powerful keys to living a joyful, rich, satisfying life while single. **Jesus is the goal, not marriage! He has a life of abundance and fullness for us right now! I believe God wants to use this book to help unlock more freedom, healing, fullness, and joy in the state of life we find ourselves in.** God truly is good and has good plans for our singleness."

   - Amber Griffioen, Youth Worker
   Cyress Center

"It's a rare gift to be able to make someone—even strangers or those on the margins of society—feel welcomed, loved, and a part of a caring community. Despite the challenges of being a single Christian female in her 30's, April has found a way to do this with grace and epitomizes how faith in action is truly lived out. **Single, married, no matter your status, April shares what's important (and what's not) when on a journey in response to the Lord's unique calling on your life.** April lives with conviction and hope, and gives of herself generously for the glory of God."

- *Shawn Plummer, President*
Food For the Hungry, Canada

"*And If I Don't* has a vital and life-giving message that people, especially in the body of Christ, need to hear and apply. **This book is rich with practical wisdom that demonstrates how to relate to and live out the single life with joy.** I believe readers will be awakened, challenged, celebrated and invited to reimagine the single life through this book."

- *Doretha Plett, Prayer Counsellor*

"April, in this book, has outlined what it is to live a life of abundance, one that Jesus promises us, while answering age old questions about what serving him in the context of marriage should look like. **Her insightful words on becoming a co-creator with God in our life story give us hope in the waiting and discerning God's will in our lives, marriage included.** As you read this, may you be encouraged to examine your lives deeper and be ready for God to take his rightful place in your life."

- *Ashish Joseph, Worship Leader*
Redemption Church

REIMAGINING THE SINGLE LIFE

April Klassen

Copyright © 2021 April Klassen

Cover design & illustrations © 2021 Kiah Ward, of Inklings Creative Collective (inklingscreativeco.ca)

Formatting and layout by Jadon Dick

All rights reserved. No portion of this book may be reproduced, stored in a retrieval system, or transmitted in any form or media or by any means, electronic, mechanical, photocopying, recording, or otherwise, without the prior written permission of the publisher. If you would like to use material from the book (other than for review purposes), prior written permission must be obtained by contacting the publisher at info@schleitheimpress.ca.

Published by:

SCHLEITHEIM PRESS

www.SchleitheimPress.com

Schleitheim Press is an imprint of
Okanagan Publishing House
1024 Lone Pine Court
Kelowna, BC V1P 1M7
www.okanaganpublishinghouse.ca

Scripture quotations are from the ESV® Bible (The Holy Bible, English Standard Version®) copyright © 2001 by Crossway, a publishing ministry of Good News Publishers. Used by permission. All rights reserved.

Printed in the United States of America

Library and Archives Canada Cataloguing in Publication
Title: And if I don't? : reimagining the single life / April Klassen.
Other titles: And if I do not
Names: Klassen, April, author.
Identifiers: Canadiana (print) 2022014477X | Canadiana (ebook) 20220145105 | ISBN 9781990389009 (softcover) | ISBN 9781990389023 (HTML)
Subjects: LCSH: Single people. | LCSH: Single people—Religious life. | LCSH: Marriage—Religious aspects—Christianity. | LCSH: Interpersonal relations—Religious aspects—Christianity. | LCSH: Contentment—Religious aspects—Christianity. | LCSH: Christian life.
Classification: LCC BV4596.S5 K53 2022 | DDC 248.8/4—dc23

1st Edition, August 2021

10   9   8   7   6   5   4   3   2   1

ISBN: 978-1-990389-00-9

Author Dedication:

To the family I was born into: Tim, Amy and Steph: What a wild and beautiful ride we've had together.

To the family around the globe that has embraced me simply because we belong to each other: You have shown me what the dinner table is supposed to look like.

To my beloved mother, Virginia: I will always be grateful for your love. Soon is never close enough.

CONTENTS

About **Food For The Hungry**..viii

Foreword...ix

Chapter One: ~~When~~ **If**... 1

Chapter Two: **Waiting**..13

Chapter Three: **Squandered**..27

Chapter Four: **Stop Shopping**... 43

Chapter Five: **Start Creating**... 59

Chapter Six: **Deliberate**..71

Chapter Seven: **S.E.X.**..91

Chapter Eight: **I'm Not Single**..107

About FOOD FOR THE HUNGRY

As a lifelong advocate for the vulnerable, April is donating a portion of the proceeds from *And If I Don't?* to Food for the Hungry's work supporting women in Bangladesh.

Food for the Hungry is a Christian non-profit organization dedicated to ending poverty - one community at a time. Recognizing that each community faces unique challenges as well as advantages, Food for the Hungry is committed to an integrated, holistic approach to development including priorities such as agriculture, education, health, and gender equality.

In Bangladesh, Food for the Hungry staff walk with community leaders to create a future where families help their neighbours and rally together to meet the needs of the entire community.

Proceeds from this book will invest in women's leadership skills through Savings Groups, where women are empowered to plan for their family's future, manage their finances, and even start their own businesses.

Learn more at: www.fhcanada.org/partner/klassen

Foreword

This is a great book. I am the author's father. I would ask you to consider that second statement not as a reason to dismiss my evaluation because of bias but to motivate you to pick up and read this book (paper or electronic) precisely because of my insider knowledge.

You have probably had the experience of hearing someone speak on a subject or read what they've written only to find out later that the principles they promoted were not exactly lived out in their own personal life. Disappointing. Their walk didn't match their talk.

I have had the privilege of knowing April her whole life from childhood to adulthood and along the way have watched her live out singleness in relationship with God in a truly remarkable and inspiring way. It is not unusual at all for me to hear glorious comments about April from people who have experienced her enthusiasm for life and her joy. I can truly vouch for her integrity and authenticity.

There's another reason I think this is a great book. I am a pastor and I have had numerous conversations with both singles and marrieds in the church. As I examine typical perspectives on marriage and singleness against Scripture we have too often diverted from God's perspective and taken on our culture's view of these. April makes a case for reimagining the single life from a scriptural standpoint in a way that is accessible and honouring to both marriage and singleness.

Lastly, I think this is a great book because it offers hope. I was married for 32 years but find myself single again due to the loss of my wife. While singleness might not be what many of us desire, 50%+ of us in the church family find ourselves in this place. If the gold standard is marriage, singles are doomed to feel second rate at best. April presents a needful corrective that infuses hope for the single without diminishing the beauty of marriage.

In the time when April was finishing up her manuscript, I was on a walk with a friend who I would consider to be a godly man. We were talking about family and I told him that April was writing a book about singleness and how to live that well before God. "Oh," he said, "she's making lemonade out of lemons." My jaw dropped ... and I said ... "THAT is why we need this book!" May "If I Don't" help you to *reimagine the single life* God's way.

- Tim Klassen, Lead Pastor, Central Heights Church

CHAPTER ONE

when, if

The woman behind the ticket counter motioned us forward. Despite my visible anticipation, I waited until my sister and her husband had collected their pre-purchased vouchers before making my way up. I had not been to a symphony orchestra in ages and it was hard not to be enamoured by the atmosphere in the building. Not only were people dressed up more than normal, but the ceilings were framed with gold plaster, crown molding, and adorned with ornate hand painted trim. A rare sort of craftsmanship in our current age of minimalism and Marie Kondo.

I was greeted at the counter by thick glasses and overly glossy lips which thankfully were hidden by an equally glossy window.

"April Klassen?" The woman questioned as she peered at my ID and then back at me through the hardly transparent glass. "And who else?"

"Um, just me." I answered.

"Are you picking up just one ticket?" She questioned again, as though she had misheard.

"That's right" I replied, "Just the one ticket please."

She began shuffling through the small brown box in front of her before repeating once more: "So, just for one. You are alone? You don't have anyone with you?"

She rather shook her head as though her question were a statement.

Was my request the first of its kind she had heard all day?

"I only bought one ticket," I re-emphasized, beginning to feel rather singled out. What was this? *Bridget Jones's Diary?* Pasting on a smile I took the ticket from the small drop bin and dashed over to where my clan was waiting for me on the side. "*Sheesh!*"

For some reason, my interaction with this woman came back to me later in the week. It was not because I was upset over the rather comical exchange, but more because it highlighted for me, that no matter how confident I am in my relationship status the world is always going to tell me something is missing.

And right now, that thing is a person.

Anyone who has been single for a while can tell you that this is a narrative we hear all around us. It's in the shows we watch, the songs we listen to and in the conversations we engage in. I am not a victim to the story I have been told, but I do live and breathe in a culture which tells me the direction my life *needs* to head towards. One that includes a significant other. Unashamedly, there are times I have bought into this lie. And when I do, I too begin to feel that something is missing. Most often this is to my own detriment.

I wish I could say that in the church we are immune to telling this story which, even if communicated indirectly, places relationship status at the center of a young person's life pursuits. But experience tells me that we have a long way to go. I have not reached the age of 34 without having felt this pressure.

I love the church. I grew up in a healthy Christian community with a family that never pushed me to get married, and for this I am grateful. But even so, I could not escape the sense that my best life included a husband and a biological family that he and I would make together. It is usually the first question I am asked when I return from a trip, start a new class, or join a new church.

"Are there any interesting men? Surely you have met someone by now! I still cannot believe someone has not come along yet. Just hang on, it'll happen when you least expect it."

But do they ever wonder if maybe I am not expecting it, or perhaps not even pursuing it?

The question, for me, has never been whether I think marriage is beautiful or whether it is biblical. I believe family was designed by God, and marriage is an incredible gift to those who find a life partner to serve him with. I have seen this modelled wonderfully for me throughout my life in very personal and tangible ways. But when you hit the age of 30, and the numbers continue to rise, it is incredible how what *could* be your life and what *isn't* tends to make you reflect on what a whole-hearted life lived for Christ should truly look like. What components are a *must*, and what components are simply *potentials*. If I decide to spend my time chasing after potentials, I fear that it is the *musts* that will suffer most.

This I know for sure: Scripture gives us more than hints at what an abundant life might look like, one that is marked by love for God, sacrifice for others, praise, pursuit of Kingdom dreams and most importantly, a life truly satisfied by Jesus.

"Love the Lord your God with all your heart, with all your soul and with all your mind. This is the great and first commandment. And a second is like it: You shall love your neighbour as yourself."
- Matthew 22:37-39

"He has told you, O man, what is good;
and what does the Lord require of you
but to do justice, and to love kindness,
and to walk humbly with your God?" - Micah 6:8

"Blessed are those who dwell in your house,
ever singing your praise!" - Psalm 84:4

"Seek first the kingdom of God and his righteousness, and all these things will be added to you." - Matthew 6:33

"For he satisfies the longing soul,
and the hungry soul he fills with good things." - Psalm 107:9

When we choose to live the way of Jesus, we find ourselves recipients of his love, and we love him and his creation in return. Through sacrifice and commitment birthed out of this place of being so deeply cared for, we bring glory to the *one* who created us in his image. We ARE living full lives. Beautiful lives. And especially when we do this in community, as Scripture so clearly guides us, we do not fall short of our calling to reflect his character, his saving power, and his goodness in our world.

But no matter how good and true this picture of a beautiful life might be, there is still a problem: *What we see and hear in our culture conveys that this is simply not enough.* Hollywood has shown us that it is not sufficient to save the world in stretchy synthetics while flying through the air. The feeling that the world is finally at peace again only really hits us when the heroic character taps on his lover's window and, at last, they can be together again. It is the concluding fireworks over the kissing couple, the final proposal, the fated run-in at the top of the Empire State Building. Everything will be alright WHEN the love story comes together. And in the rare tragedies where this does not happen, there is still a sense of love had, tried for, or lost. And our hearts hurt for the poor characters who did not get the "best ending" possible.

Recently I had to laugh, as I watched the newest remake of the classic story *Little Women*. The tale, which takes place in America in the 1860's, profiles the journey of a young Jo March. Ambitious, stubborn, and set to make something of her life apart from an early marriage like her eldest sister, Jo ventures off to New York to widen her horizons. Her passion to write lands Jo several publications in the local newspaper, though none convey her true writing talents. When she finally writes about something she believes in - her own story and that of her family - the publisher stops her part way through her script, demanding to know which gentleman marries the main character in the story. Jo relays to the publisher that the character will not marry, and that he should have picked up on this by then. After all, the character has explained throughout the entire novel that she intends to remain single. The publisher sneers at her, offering his most sincere advice: to make the book a love story. No one, in his opinion, will buy a book in which the heroine is a spinster. It's not what people want to hear, and it certainly won't guarantee them any book sales.

Despite Jo's visible disgust at the admonishment, the movie ends minutes later with the budding author at long last in the arms of her German professor. All is made right after all. And the story sells.

So if this is the story Hollywood would tell us, what reels are being played in our churches? Is the tale we tell ourselves hinging on the moment *when* our significant other enters the picture? Is that truly when things are going well for us? Because if so, this leaves us at a loss if that occurrence never happens. How easily we can interpret this as having missed out on the apex of our stories.

If the mark of a life well lived orbits around this kind of love story, one that declares we *will have* or even *deserve to have* a partner in life, then I fear that we have set ourselves up for failure. For as much as we sing that "Jesus is enough," the questions we ask each other, the opportunities we have categorized as loss, and the singular lens of celebration of romantic relationships so often portrays a different story in our communities. And by doing so, we are hurting not only ourselves, but a generation who has yet to ask what their best life should look like. We are giving them an amended version. Because if my best life can only be achieved when I reach marriage, my failure to attain this reinforces that *something is wrong with me.* It persuades me that people have disappointed me and even more so, God has let me down. Shouldn't he know what my best life is missing?

I have seen over and over again how this view of singleness leads to hasty marriages, depression and feelings of inadequacy. It can cause us to become dissatisfied with the incredible ways God is at work in and around us, simply because we are focused on the one area where we do not see his intervention.

So many of these thoughts are circulating in our churches and yet, somehow, we fail to see that we have made marriage the goal not a gift.

A life well lived is not simply marked by movement towards marriage, *but towards Christ*. If this is true, then the partners we have or do not have on the way are not what characterize our success or failure. As wonderful as they might be, they are not what bring us our greatest joy: Jesus is.

But are we ready to change the way we speak about marriage? Can we embrace a life that replaces *when* with *if*? Because truly that is a life surrendered. It is also a life of possibility. If our churches embraced loving our community towards deeper relationship with Jesus and with one another, celebrating equally the gifts of marriage and the gifts of singleness, perhaps we could be a little more convinced that this was so.

I am not just addressing here the messages we preach to our congregations on marriage, family and singleness, for I *do* think there has been a shift over time by many churches to accommodate the needs and wants of growing numbers of singles in our current cultural moment. After all, as represented by a 2019 Statistics Canada study, the number of Canadian adults living alone has doubled in the past 35 years.[1] *Doubled.* Our churches have looked for ways to accommodate the needs of this growing demographic, and rightly so. Singles groups are one of the ways they have done this, extending the age of young adults way past 25 years etc.

---

1 Weikle, Brandie. "More Canadians Live Alone Than Ever Before: StatsCan Report." *Canadian Broadcasting Corporation.* 2019.

But accommodating the shift in changing demographics has not really impacted the ways we speak about marriage and continue to project the best course of life for the young believer. We are more comfortable to tell a longing heart that their turn is next or 'someday', than to dream about what another kind of life might look like. *"If you don't get married, these are some of the amazing things God might be preparing for you..."* It is the smallest change of wording, but the implications are huge!

I love words, and I love how changing a sentence by adjusting one word can make such a significant difference, how it can mean something entirely different.

I learned French when I was 18 and travelled to France as a nanny. If I thought English had some challenging concepts to it, French was a whole new ballgame. Masculine, feminine, a million rules with a million exceptions to the rules. And I found it all fascinating. And at times embarrassing!

On one occasion my use of the English word 'hot' to describe the temperature of the room we were in had an entire dinner table laughing at my distorted knowledge of the word's grammatical implications. I will spare you the details. However, my red face clearly portrayed that 'heat' was not too far stretched of a word choice.

Replacing one word can change the entire framework of what we are communicating. A confirmation can become a possibility. Patterns can be broken leaving room to explore. When I suggest that we replace *when* with *if*, I am suggesting the use of a conditional clause. This provides us with a different framework to ponder the course of direction we map out so readily to our youth, and even to ourselves. *If,* leaves room to ponder, to analyze, to think outside a predestined path. *If,* indicates that other ways are possible, that the opposite might be true, even chosen, and I would go as far as to emphasize, *celebrated.*

"*If* you get married…"

Means that equally plausible is:

"*If* you don't get married…"

Suddenly there is room to imagine. A life outside of marriage? What would that even look like? Would it be easier? Harder? Lonely? Satisfying? *More exciting?*

I never heard this growing up. I am sure it was assumed it could be a possibility, but it was never vocalized. Furthermore, observing the celebrations around me, I just absorbed the idea that we were all going to get married one day. My sisters, my friends, my schoolmates.

Our practices of celebrating every aspect on the journey towards marriage do not go unnoticed. We celebrate engagements, weddings, and the resulting baby showers. There is a market for these sorts of celebrations, as anyone who has been in a wedding or who has helped plan one can testify. Add wedding, to any sticker label and the price of the item is sure to double. Wedding photos, wedding decorations, wedding invitations; items and services offering the same outcomes are suddenly worthy of cashing in family inheritances and stock shares. There is a market for love!

One of my family's favorite movies is *Father of The Bride*. In the film, comedian Steve Martin nearly goes insane while assisting his beloved only daughter in putting together and paying for a rather extravagant home wedding. The wedding cake, as he so kindly reminds the wedding coordinator, costs as much as his first car. Never mind the swans, tents, parking attendants etc.

As overdone and elaborate as the scenes in the movie are, the film points out the extent to which he and his wife have dreamed of this occasion, this wedding, for their daughter since she was a child. Their only daughter, *a bride*. Despite Steve Martin believing his daughter is too young to get married, he knows it was only a matter of time.

My family has had our own chuckles over the movie, as a unit with three girls. We actually watched Father of the Bride before each of my sisters' weddings. There is just a slight resemblance of Steve Martin's character, George Banks, to the quirky and financially astute father of ours, despite our doubtfulness that he would ever end up in jail for stealing hot-dog buns!

We celebrate marriage. In our families. In our churches. And we should. It is a powerful message that communicates covenant, commitment, sacrifice and deep love. It should and often does point us to the sacrificial love of Jesus for his bride. And I will not lie, I have loved watching my sisters and close friends get married. Seeing the strength of partnership that they share with their husbands is powerful. The shared pursuit of Jesus, so central to their lives, is a really beautiful thing.

But I hope we would still see their journey towards Christ as equally beautiful *if* they had not met their husbands. *If* they had continued to pursue the heart of the Father for themselves and for the world around them, no matter whether or not their hands bore a ring.

I remember driving home last year from a fun evening out with a great guy I'd met a few months earlier. We laughed, had inspiring conversation, and ate a lot of good food. We had so much in common, it was crazy.

And yet, my drive home that night was miserable. Rain mixed with a steady flow of tears that blurred my view of the future as I processed where my heart was at. Everything about this guy said: "Give him a chance". Our worldviews, our love for Jesus, even some of our particular passions and hobbies had a striking resemblance. Surely, together we could make a big impact on the world. And it would be nice to have a partner.

And yet, my heart felt nothing.

I could not think of any character flaws that should have pushed me away from this relationship. I actually could not think of any reason why it shouldn't work.

What was wrong with me?

Once arriving home, I wiped off my runny mascara, put on my pajamas and sat on the couch staring blankly at the empty fireplace as though it was lit.

A well-intentioned friend drove over later that night and gave me a giant hug before turning to say: "You know, one day you will understand why this didn't work out. When you meet the right guy, you will know. You'll look back and laugh at this whole thing."

But will I?

What I really needed in that moment was not someone telling me that marriage was still on the table. Because in that moment, it was not. And a year later, it is still not looking that way. It is not to say that things can't change, that we shouldn't pray for marriage if it is something we desire. But neither do we need to reinforce that the roads we are on will only lead us in one direction.

I do not always need reminders that *when* I get married it will all make sense. Because what if it does not? Does that mean none of it is worth it? Sometimes in the *ifs* we just need to know that certain things are not. And I continue to learn more of who I turn to in my greatest joys and my deepest nights of weeping: the *one* who is constant, unchanging, and ever so faithful.

What I needed that late Sunday night was simply someone to cry with. The relationship not working out did not mean that another one would. It just meant that I was no longer dating.

And one year later, I am totally okay with that.

CHAPTER TWO

waiting

I have never been a fan of waiting. And I am not the only one in my family. Anyone who knows me and my eldest sister knows that, even if we have invited you to join our team for a run (the Vancouver SunRun, the Run for Water, the East Van 10km... you name it!), we are racing for speed. About 40 seconds into the race, we'll look at each other, look at our group and then take off. Well, we might first ask "Do you mind if we just run ahead?" And the looks we receive from the first-year team members always remind me that some people actually think we are going to run the entire race together. *"Surely,"* I tell myself, *"Surely, they knew..."* Thankfully my sister and I are both competitive, and we hold a similar pace. But just don't ask us to wait. PLEASE!

There is something about getting where you desire to go and not feeling held back by anything. The speed. The rush. It's exhilarating.

I hate waiting.

I hate waiting to make decisions. If something seems like the best option, I say *"Let's go, let's try it. What is the worst that can happen?*" I find shopping with analytical friends one of the most excruciating exercises on earth. Every pair of jeans they try on look great. Do they really need to sit on it for an hour, go back twice and then wear them at home for a week with the tags still on to make sure they are the right pair? It is a good thing I have not had to shop the housing market yet. That would be disastrous!

I also hate waiting for circumstances to change. I love reading, but some books have such a slow buildup to the climax it is irritating. My book club recently read *A Gentleman in Moscow* by Amor Towles.[1] The novel features a young Russian influencer who has been sentenced to live the remainder of his life inside the four walls of a famous hotel in Moscow. Well as you can probably guess, the lack of physical room to meander means the story contains little action, and a plethora of character development. As much as I love character progression, every reader, in my humble opinion, reaches a point where you do not care what colour the principal character's mustache is. I will admit on several occasions I skipped ahead a few pages (or maybe chapters) to see what pivotal moments might be around the corner. The suspense of everyday life was killing me. Plus, I decided, my book club did not need to know I had read ahead. We would all arrive at the same conclusion at the end!

While it can be hard to wait for a book's conclusion, waiting for our life circumstances to change is a little more difficult. There are no pages to flip, only choices to be made, and sometimes it seems we are making these choices in the dark. We know where we would *like* our stories to go, but we do not know if that is

---

[1] Towles, Amor. *A Gentleman in Moscow*. Viking Press, 2016.

really where we will end up. And truth be told, sometimes we do not even know if our choices will make a difference.

What if our choices only lead to more waiting? More pain. More silence. What then?

Well, throughout the past few years, God has spoken to me on numerous occasions about waiting.

As much as I have struggled, and potentially always will, to understand a holistic view of waiting, he has made a couple things just a bit clearer.

1. *Waiting can hold virtue.*

2. *Waiting can be a crutch.*

How I wait, and what I am waiting on, shows the truest desires of my heart. It is at the core of my journey with the Father. And because of this, I am beginning to understand that waiting is of great importance to the Lord. His patience is unfathomable. It is enduring, so that all might come to repentance and saving faith. It is consistent, in that everyday I can hear him calling me to return to him with all my heart and give my affections to him. And just as he has demonstrated this kind of persistent love for us, he has shown that in our own lives he has called us to surrender our own agendas and time frames and listen to his direction for our lives.

How I wait, and what I am waiting on makes all the difference.

I have heard him whisper to me over the years these instructions in different areas of my life:

"Do not wait."

"Wait."

"Wait actively."

And a new cycle begins.

I cannot stress the richness and need in our lives for more of the Holy Spirit. The comforter, the one who brings conviction, who leads us into understanding. The third person of the Trinity brings an incredible vibrancy to the meaning of my every day. I cannot imagine an existence without him.

As I look back over the years, I see how it is the Holy Spirit who has graciously brought awareness to the ebbs and flows of my life. Of my rest and my restlessness. My action and my pause. My movement and my stillness. My planning and my trust. And, as with any good parent, he has been showing me that on some things he has called me to wait, while for others in that waiting I am simply wasting time. At times he has reminded me that things I am waiting on, whether for myself or for a friend, are holding me back from the greater thing he wants me to move towards. In these places he has challenged me to stop waiting. Most importantly I am learning that in different seasons, the stopping and going, the waiting and the contending will change. What is constant is that he is faithful to be there with me, and he wants to lead me.

When I was graduating from high school, the list of things I was waiting for was quite long. I hoped the years ahead of me would provide opportunities to travel, a career that I would love and financial stability leading to fiscal freedom. I wanted to move out and start a life of my own. Go to university. And of course I just assumed, along that process, there would come a life partner. Maybe not too early on, as I wanted some independence first. But eventually.

Well, opportunities did come up for me to travel. In fact, the next 15 years of my life became full of incredibly rich experiences overseas. I worked in 12 different countries in between and after completing a degree in International Studies. I did move out. Albeit non-profit does not really set you up for total financial freedom, but it did provide me with a career path I loved and thrived in. The long list of things I had hoped to accomplish or find eventually did come to pass.

All except one.

I am 34, and I still desire one day to be married. It is not that this longing has gone away, nor do I believe that it will. But a question I have had to ask myself is this: *"Do I let that desire control me, or do I allow my desire for Jesus to become greater? Do I feed or nurture the desire to be in God's presence more than I do the desire for a husband?"*

I do not address this area of longing lightly, for I know that it can be a deeply painful area for many singles. Especially when so many of us have grown up believing that the "best life" includes, one day, marriage. The grief we can experience, at times, grows alongside over-due expectations. And questions from well-intentioned people do not always help.

"You are how old and not yet married?"

I remember laughing when asked this question often during my travels through Bangladesh, Burundi, Turkey, and some of the other beautiful countries I have worked in. In many of these places women marry and begin families at extremely young ages. The average age of first pregnancy is shockingly younger than even my 'city-in-the-country' hometown of Abbotsford, BC. Many of the women I met in my early 20's had four to eight children already. Meeting me and finding out that I was unattached, and childless, was simply unfathomable. And then the questions really started…

Now, I realize very well that our expectations of age and family numbers vary greatly from country to country. Most people in Canada do not laugh or stare when they hear that I am unattached and childless, but neither does our culture shy away from projecting lifestyles that make singles feel they just do not quite fit the mold.

Truth be told, we should not be trying to fit into a mold.

When I look back on my life, I don't think I would trade a day in my single life during my 20's to have married. My heart overflows with memories from the people I have met and the places I have been. I could write numerous books about them and not run out of stories.

I can truly say that, most of the time, I have sincerely loved and embraced the single life.

But I do not *always* feel that way, and that is okay too.

There are days when I feel like I got left behind. When, although I love still being able to go out at night, none of my closest friends can join me because they are tucking kids into bed.

There are years when I am tired of moving into yet another home, with another set of roommates. More personalities and pet peeves to figure out, cleaning cycles to plan, and food items to hide.

There are moments when I see a couple living the way I would want to, and a little burst of pain pops up, reminding me that deep down I always thought I would have that.

As singles, I do believe most of us will go through ups and downs of desires. There is a constant need to release this desire to God. To trust that he is working out, in and through us, the best story possible.

The more I seek to know who God is, the more I believe that this is true.

And the more I seek to know God, the more I realize he is what I need most, and he is worth waiting for. He never disappoints.

I made the mistake when I lived in France of showing up on time for a hangout with several of my Moroccan friends at a smoothie bar. Moroccans love smoothies. And I learned to as well.

My family makes fun of me, because every time I come back from working in a new country, I bring back a new trick, habit, or food love. In France I learned to love avocado smoothies (alongside croissants, cheeses, and a variety of other patisserie wonders). I never learned to make most of Paris' delicacies, I just did not have the patisserie skill level… but Moroccan smoothies, I could master.

Well, I first learned to love this tasty drink while waiting for my friends at a smoothie bar just a 20-minute walk from my apartment. Normally we met at their place a few metro stations away, but it was a nice change to stay closer to home. So, when they told me to join them at 6PM at their favorite café, I showed up at 5:55. I found a little table against the mirrored wall, put down my bag and walked over to the counter where I was greeted by a dark-haired man with a big smile wearing a dress. Using my newly acquired skills I placed my order in Arabic, despite butchering the pronunciation of avocado. The owner laughed, shocked to hear a French customer ordering in Arabic.

"Ah ha!", I corrected him, "But I am not French."

Clearly, I was not Moroccan either... for the clock kept ticking on and before long it was 6:15, 6:30, 6:45 - eventually the clock hit 7pm! My friends were not no-shows. They continued to text me throughout my wait:

"We have left the train."

"We are on the bus."

"Amina forgot her purse."

"We are running back... Okay, back on route."

"Almost there! Be there in 25."

My friends rolled in at around 7:30, apologizing profusely. They had completely forgotten I was not Moroccan and would actually show up on time!

From then on, I was 45 minutes late for all our meetings - the best I could do as a North American - and still sat for at least 20 minutes on my own practicing Arabic with the shop owner before my friends would show up. We were all compromising.

The thing is, meeting up with my friends, and subsequent gatherings at the smoothie shop were always worth the wait because my Moroccan friends never cancelled on me. They might have been habitually late by my standards, but they were the most faithful friends. They were always checking in on me, always coming to my work events, always calling when things were tough. So even after an hour and a half of waiting, I was sure they would come through. Now, if my North American friends had not shown up after 2 hours…

You get the picture.

It is never a waste of our time waiting on Jesus because he will never fail us. He always shows up. He might not show up in the timing that we like, or even in the ways we prefer, but we can rest assured he is with us on the way. He has gone before us, and believe it or not, he has a plan. Sometimes we just need to readjust ours.

It is so easy to fixate on the things in this life that we are waiting for with more passion than we do on Jesus. When, by our timeline, things are not going as we had hoped, we can easily become consumed by the thoughts of how to make them happen, how desperately we want them.

A friend of mine in Lithuania shared with me about a very dark time in her life. While attending a New Year's party with friends, a hurtful comment made by one of the young couples about her singleness sent Skaidra reeling into depression. She began to question God, and his plans for her life. Why would he let her reach her late 20's without meeting anyone? Most of her friends were married and she felt a pressure to be in the same stage of life. She longed for a partner. She was lonely and tired of comments from others about how to meet someone and what she should do, how she was not trying hard enough. She made a vow to God after the party: If she was not in a relationship by her 27th birthday, just one year from then, she would kill herself. And the clock began ticking.

Skaidra is now 36. She is an incredible woman of God whom I look up to in so many ways. I am so thankful she has lived to tell her story. Skaidra is not married, and her life is joyful, vibrant, and full of meaning. You can see in the process of such deep pain and disappointment how the Holy Spirit was at work in Skaidra's heart. He began to show her that he had not abandoned her because she was single. Just as he had not abandoned those who could not have children, or whose spouses died, or who lost their health. Skaidra's frustration and disappointment stemmed from wanting marriage more than she wanted God. Marriage was becoming an idol in her life. The one thing she was willing to live for or die without.

We all have idols. Some idols are easy to see, others look a little more like good things, even great things. Still, they are things that we have made too much of. We can idolize our time, our money, our status. We can idolize marriage or kids.

We know idols have popped up in our lives when the very things we want, the gifts we think God should give us, become more desirable to us than him.

What Jesus created us to pursue and wait on is him, his presence. This is greater than anything we could desire or seek with our lives, be it career, money, beauty, or a life partner.

And the hold these things might have over us only loosens when we are filled with the power and presence of God.

In our desire for something, release is found in the pursuit of *someone*. And it is in that space that our deepest transformation occurs.

I learned this lesson during a very unique season in my own life.

Shortly after my 26th birthday, my mom was diagnosed with kidney cancer. It was serious enough that I left my job in Montreal and flew back to my family's home near Vancouver to journey with them through her illness. The 9 months that ensued were painfully hard, though still not as challenging as the days of her absence following her death.

Throughout mom's sickness we always believed it was possible her cancer might disappear. She could be healed. And I, along with my family, prayed and waited on God to do something. I knew that I needed to hold this request with an open hand. Yet I prayed with faith, knowing nothing was impossible for the creator of the universe.

It was painful watching my mom slowly die, because the desire of my heart was to keep her with me.

During the 9 months of pills, surgeries and visits to the doctor, my family decided together that we would press into the only thing we knew could help us through this. More than friends, family, or podcasts, we needed to be in God's presence.

I have never prayed, worshipped, or journaled as much as I did that year. Neither do I believe I have ever felt the presence of God in such tangible ways. The more I sought Jesus, the more my desire for him grew. And as this love from and for him filled my heart, he began to shift the way I was praying, leading me to pray in ways that were less self-focused than I had been praying before. They were not as centered around mom's healing, despite continuing to pray for her with fervour. There was nothing wrong with my prayers, but as I began to feel more of the Father's heart, I realized there was so much more I could pray for. As my eyes turned outwards, I began to see how the Lord was moving around me in amazing ways.

I never stopped praying for my mom, but my perspective on the situation changed, because I no longer was asking and waiting for God to do something for me. I was pleading and waiting for more of God.

Pain is not something many of us ask for. And yet, for those of us who desire marriage and have not received this gift, there can be pain. There is heartache at not having a dream fulfilled that was longed for, prayed for, and anticipated. Sometimes it can even feel like a dream we were clinging to has died.

It is okay to grieve the things we longed for. I have grieved deeply for the loss of my mom. I have learned to grieve with friends over other kinds of losses. The Psalms are full of grieving and crying out to God. But so often through that process, the crying out, if it is truly directed to God, leads us deeper into his presence. In his presence there is comfort, there is healing, and there begins to be a stirring in our hearts of wonder at the source of it all. And it leads us to worship. This is transformation. As we begin to wait on Jesus, bringing him our dreams, our burdens, our longings, we begin to realize that more than anything, he is truly what we want.

So where do you sit in your timeline of waiting? What are the things you feel you have been waiting for, waiting on?

I do not want to suggest that we stop crying out to God for good things that our hearts desire. But I do want to suggest that we choose not to put a limit on God's ways, which are higher than ours. If we believe that he is the best we can have, then we can pray for the things we desire with open hands.

We can praise him amid unfulfilled dreams, standing in wonder of who he is, even while being unsure of how he is working. We can wait actively and be deeply satisfied.

"Satisfy us in the morning with your steadfast love" - Psalm 90:14.

When Jesus departed from his disciples, he did not promise that their lives would look the way they wanted. He did not prophesy over them houses filled with children and comfort. He knew that life was going to be hard. He knew that they would suffer and ache and yearn for things that they would never have. But more importantly, he promised to be with them. Always.

No love is as deep or as wide or as high as the love of our Saviour and if we let him love us, we will know a love stronger than any human love we could ever desire. He is GOOD to us.

The more we bring our desires to Jesus and turn our eyes to him, the more our hearts begin to worship and the more our hearts become satisfied. It is it in this place of worship that waiting begins to feel different. The things that we sought after more than Jesus begin to die.

And in Christ, where there is death there is also resurrection.

When we release to the Father our desires, our hopes, the dreams of how we thought our lives would look, and we turn to him for comfort, he will strengthen us. And in the death of our idols, the release of our dreams, and the promises we have so often told ourselves must come true, he will begin to birth something new.

Our world needs young people who know the resurrection power of Jesus in their stories. Men and women who have said yes to releasing their dreams, so that he can give them new ones. For those who have dreamed of marriage, this does not mean that marriage will not happen one day. It might.

But the point is that there will be release.

God is calling men and women who have said yes *to him*, not just *his gifts*. And the reward of following Jesus is far greater.

CHAPTER THREE

Squandered

When COVID-19 broke out, the entire world stopped. Everything shut down. Nothing was moving. No one was really supposed to be moving around, unless (in Canada) you were on a bike getting fresh air, or you were a health care worker, or strangely enough, a construction worker (I guess the need for new living spaces after quarantining effects on roommates emerged was enough to consider this an essential service!).

But whatever your profession was, life totally changed.

With work going online, many of us web-cammed in our pajamas, we learned to grocery shop only once a week despite increased snacking, and our social lives took on new forms or completely paused.

I think it is safe to say that with most restaurants closed and crowded spaces and gatherings prohibited, most people found themselves at home in the evenings. Gone were the expectations to be somewhere, doing something. The only expectation was to stay home.

This was hard for many of us who have bought into the cultural lie that says we must be busy, that *"unbusy people are unimportant people."* Normally we pursue things that fill our time using our connections, our money, and our freedom. And yet, there we were early in 2020 with the sudden cultural demands of 'busy' being lifted off of us. We had a whole new set of parameters to navigate, and aside from parents with active toddlers and crying babies, we all had one thing in common: more time.

It is funny how when the things you are so accustomed to spending your time on are suddenly taken away, you begin to see other opportunities around you. A lack of a pursuit of a certain kind of evening leads to the pursuit of another kind. Without bars, restaurants and social events, there was reading, puzzling, baking, zoom-calling.

For some, the world became their stage.

I have never seen so many home haircuts, hour long Instagram stories and TikTok videos exploding onto social media. Friends sipping coffee to Michael Jackson beats and dancing behind bushes to Justin Bieber.

Some found alternative ways to cultivate community. Drive-by birthday parties became the thing to do. My brother-in-law dressed up in his climbing gear and taped fake mountains on his car to cruise by a 60th birthday party for a friend with whom he had once hiked the Himalayas. There were 60 cars participating in the parade. Kids cheered from their cars while driving adults dressed up in nonsense honked their horns and sang happy birthday.

Some people benefited from the extra time, playing games with family, dropping off groceries for neighbours, and exercising. And at the same time, there was a whole sector of society that found solace from the anxiety of the unknown season through Netflix and sleep. Netflix that played episodes until 3AM and sleep that made pajamas the most convenient work attire given the three rushed minutes they had to get up and switch on the web-cam for work. Forbes reported that Netflix signed up 15.8 million new global subscribers in the first quarter of 2020![1]

Except for the pizza-delivery persons and Amazon workers who dared peer through consumer windows, few people knew what really took up one another's time during the long hours spent within the confines of our homes.

Everyone had to decide for themselves how to spend this increased commodity that we all deemed so valuable.

Not surprisingly many of us began comparing the untackled to-do lists in our lives. Normally we had excuses for our inability to engage in things we consider of high priority. But even during our stay-at-home quarantine, other excuses seemed unforgivingly to pop up. What happened to the amazing opportunities we had to finally call distant relatives, to write, invent and/or study? Opportunities to dive deeper into Scripture or spend more time praying and worshipping were quickly drowned out by buzzing phone alerts, relentless Insta-stories and online Boggle matches. Who would have guessed mindless Christmas puzzles could make priorities that much more difficult? There is nothing wrong with Instagram, Boggle or puzzling, however, it shocked me how easily these little habits took the place of the greater pursuits I knew many of us really wanted to spend our time on.

---

[1] Walsh, Joe. "Netflix Subscriber Growth Slows After Surging During Pandemic." Forbes.com. 2020.

About one month, and 6 pounds after the effects of COVID-19 took over our normal rhythms of life, the thought hit me that this season was potentially once in a lifetime. I needed to decide how I was going to spend it. I could make it count, or I could let the incredible opportunities surrounding me pass me by.

One thing was certain: no matter how I viewed the situation - whether celebrating a little extra me time or mourning the normal connections of community - I would never get that time back.

We do not always choose the seasons of life that we find ourselves in, but we do choose how we live them out. We are not bystanders to our lives and yet sometimes we act as though we are sleepwalking through them. As though we will start living when things go a little more the way we desire.

If life is truly a race, as the writer in Hebrew writes (12:1-3), then we are not spectators to an incredible event. We are the racers. We throw off what hinders us, and we run.

Paul touches on this straining forward in Philippians 3:14, when he writes that we press on towards what lies ahead. We press on toward the goal. Paul is sitting in prison writing about movement towards Jesus, encouraging the church not to *stop*. He writes that we are to press on towards the prize, which is Jesus.

Paul, if anyone, had the right to sit in his jail cell and give up. This was most likely not the season he had foreseen or wanted. But he did not *squander the opportunity*, and instead he used an incredibly difficult period in his life to pen many of the inspired New Testament letters to teach and guide the churches he loved and wished to be with. Letters that for so many years now have been instrumental in the life of the global church. More than fixating on changing his present circumstances, Paul was content to see his life, his time, used for God's glory.

The choice was his.

And the choice is yours and mine.

What kind of person am I choosing to be? Am I one who squanders my time, my singleness, my life circumstances? Or have I stopped waiting for these things to change so I can pursue the dreams that God gives me as I pursue more of him?

Jesus is not looking for people who are waiting for life to look the way they thought it should before they pursue his call. Jesus is calling people who are willing now. And I hope I am one of those.

Mark 1:16-20 paints a picture for us of the kind of people Jesus invites to follow him. As he walks along the sea, Jesus sees two brothers fishing. They are going about their daily business, catching fish to sell at the market. It is most likely a normal day for them. I can almost hear the wind on the shore whistling and tossing bits of sand around Jesus' feet as he approaches Simon and Andrew. Their net is a little tangled, but they manage to pull apart the knot that has caught on another large cord and they throw the mesh of rope back into the sea. The net lands with a large splash and bubbles of water froth to the surface as the cords slowly sink to the sea floor. It is a hot, dry day in Galilee and fishermen are everywhere. People are briskly walking around Jesus, carrying pails of fish to load in the market carts. *Business as usual.* And yet, for the two brothers on the shore of the sea, everything is about to change.

"Follow me," Jesus calls to them from where they are working, "and I will make you fishers of men."

Now, if I were Simon or Andrew, my reply probably would have included a long list of questions in response to this sort of invitation. "Now? Follow you? How? Where are you going? For how long? What about our boat? Our fish? This is how I plan to make money…"

The response of Simon and Andrew seems perhaps less crazy to us in hindsight, but imagine being one of them. Jesus was asking them to leave everything they knew, their nets, the lifestyle they had perhaps envisioned for their lives. I most likely would have asked Jesus to come back after work hours so we could discuss further what exactly he was asking of me.

But Simon and Andrew did not.

Immediately, it says, they left their nets and followed Jesus.

Did they really understand what Jesus was calling them to?

The same passage explains that walking further along Jesus finds another two men. They are brothers, mending their nets in a boat floating on the same sea. When Jesus calls to them, James and John also respond to his invitation.

Both men leave their boat, with their father still working inside it, and go to Jesus.

Immediately.

It is hard to wrap my mind around this kind of response. When Jesus invites me to join him in his work, I question him. I find excuses. I get lazy. Sometimes, I even become fearful. The disciples that Jesus called to follow him had every excuse to say the timing was not right for them to leave their nets, their boats, their livelihoods and their families to follow Jesus into something they could not quite yet understand. But they did follow. They did respond. Because it was Jesus.

And they wasted no time in saying yes.

It is tempting for us to squander seasons in our lives because we feel our circumstances are not ideal, or perhaps just not what we had quite imagined. We would rather figure those things out first before we give our yes to God.

But we might miss out on the very best thing God has in store for our lives, if we cling to what *could be* instead of embracing the call he has for us *right now*.

I do not want to waste the single years of my life. Whether or not my relationship status will ever change is a mystery. But the fact that time is passing is not. I cannot regain the hours and months and years I spend if I ignore the call of God on my life for the pursuit of other things, no matter how good or appropriate they might seem to me. The call to follow Jesus might not look as though it will lead me closer to a lifestyle I had always imagined for myself. But whether or not it does is not the most important thing.

And I don't want to die silently in my bed watching Netflix when there is so much more right outside my door.

I want to give Jesus my yes. A life surrendered to his calling. One that says "I will follow you, wherever that takes me, however that looks. Single, married, widowed, I still have a choice to make."

Sometimes this feels easier than at other times. Sometimes my community makes me feel better for it, and at other times, it does not.

When I was preparing to go overseas to work with a mission organization at the age of 27, I had several people hint that the life choices I was making likely would not lead me towards marriage. Was I okay with that?

Jesus had not given a clear word to me about marriage at that time in my life. What he had shown me was what the next steps in my life were to look like. And right then it looked like getting on a plane, saying goodbye to my friends and family, and joining a different family on the other side of the globe for a few years. I knew the place I was going to had far fewer believers than where I was currently living. I knew the church was comprised mostly of young women and the chances of meeting a husband overseas seemed lower than in our large North American churches in Canada. But that was not why I felt called to go. God had given me incredible freedom as a single to serve him with a specific capacity and with certain gifts that he wanted to use right then in a specific place, for a specific season. Not later. He was telling me: "Now."

Immediately.

I recall hearing the words of the Father echoing in my head as I prepared to leave. *"Put aside the things that hinder, that weigh you down. Run your race. No one else's. This is the race I have set before you, so run with all your heart. Don't look beside you or behind. Don't squander time, comparing your stride to other racers. I am the prize and I am in front of you, so run to me."*

I was encouraged when I joined my team in France to work with some families and a few other singles. One of my teammates Sean, shared with me an article he wrote entitled Singleness and Unicorns. In it, he described his frustration at being one of only two single men in our entire mission's organization who was serving overseas, despite seeing dozens of young single women being commissioned and sent off.

In Sean's words:

> "I often hear people saying that they want to do missions eventually, but they want to do it after they have completed their little list. They want to settle down first, they want to get out of debt, they want to find a spouse, buy a house, start a family, and find some financial security. Once the list is done, they will move overseas, but only when the list has been all checked. What is that saying about the "best laid plans of mice and men…"?
>
> I would be lying if I said that I didn't have at least some of those same thoughts. But I realized that those things might never come to pass unless I try to force them. The singleness thing for example: it is not my dream to remain single the rest of my life. I would love to get married and to have a family. I really enjoy being in a relationship, but I am not going to force the matter; settle for someone who does not have the same dream and vision of serving my Lord overseas. I am not laying down my call because I am single.
>
> I have also made the decision that I am not going to let my singleness hold me back. My relationship status does not dictate my life in relationship with God; my life in relationship with God dictates what I do and where I go, no matter my status. I want to embrace the adventure that God has for me.

I want to give it 100% right where I am at this moment. I would rather live a life of adventure with God as a single, than sitting at home on my parents' couch waiting for the right girl to come along or trying to check off that list.

So, here I am, a single guy living in the "most romantic city in the world", "the city of love" itself, and I don't regret it at all. My friends say that they will visit Paris when they are married. Some say they feel bad because I am in such a romantic city as a single, I cannot be here with my wife. But I do not have a wife, and neither do they, so what are they waiting for? Only God knows if I will ever have a wife and a family, but I am not going to sit on the sidelines of life just because I don't know. If I wait for all the stars to align, and for every piece of the puzzle to fit together perfectly odds are I would never go."

Sean and I had many hilarious conversations about working overseas as singles. We had completely opposite personalities, and we needed each other's gifts in our team. While I was super outgoing and boisterous in creating team activities and programs, Sean was quiet and picked up on many of the little details I was sure to miss. Along with the families and other singles in our team, we were each called to pursue the kingdom as like-minded followers of Jesus, bringing our contributions to the table. We did not always do this perfectly, especially given the many other personalities of our team thrown into the mix... but grace was a word we all had to learn as we gave the ministry our everything.

People that I have served alongside in my life have helped me to keep running when I do not feel like it anymore. Sometimes, I just feel tired and tempted to become complacent in how I spend my time as a single. I love 'me' time. I have plenty of hobbies that bring me joy, but I do not need to do them all the time.

My non-church friends applaud me for being a happy single. But when they begin explaining their understanding of why I should embrace the single life, I realize that we are not quite on the same page.

Our world tells us that the freedom in being single should be channelled towards fulfilling our every desire. We should capitalize on every perk. I mean, if you think about it, as singles, we can travel unconstrained, focus on self-improvement, spend our money on ourselves and have multiple partners with no strings attached. Our minds are less cluttered, less focused on resolving problems and fixing fights with our partners. Decisions about work, moving, holidays… they rest in our hands with no need for input. There are so many reasons to be single, so many opportunities to grab hold of!

Several colleagues I have worked with have bemoaned the fact they got married. They wish it were easier to have other partners on the side without their spouses finding out. They should have kept separate bank accounts, so their partners' spending habits would not affect their long-term savings plans. The freedom of being single, to some of them, far outweighs the duties of marriage.

But I must ask myself, is this kind of freedom supposed to be a good thing?

Despite loving to travel and plan my own weekends, it is not hard for me to see how our world's guide to the single life falls so short of a life well lived. The freedom I have in Christ does not equate to the freedoms our world says are to be grabbed at. Living in a covenant relationship with Jesus does not mean I pursue all the freedoms of my culture, but neither does it mean my life as a single will be any less exciting or rewarding.

The years I have had as a single, adventuring with God, have been anything but dull. I realize that in part, this is due to perspective. And in periods where I find myself caught up in routine and perceived lack, I realize it is *I* who am missing the bigger picture of God's greatness and the joy he has for me, even in the simple day to day things of ordinary life.

Being unattached does not necessarily mean I have to go work overseas or live like Mother Teresa to say I have embraced God's call for me. I do not need to run myself into exhaustion to say that I am running the race. I am not suggesting that we replace the idols of selfishness, fear or laziness with a new idol of "working for God," to earn his approval or love. However, I do want to suggest that as we commune with God we will find the passions of his heart motivating us in the way we live our lives, and in the way we embrace opportunities around us.

We do not need to say yes to everything. We do, however, need to consider whether God deserves our yes. Because if he does, we might find that he calls our names more often than we have listened for.

I often hear singles critique marriage or see its downfall as the all-consuming hours spent on caring for children and husbands and wives. To some extent this might be true. And we see in Scripture how Paul commends and hopes for more in the church to be single, just as he is, for these exact reasons. However, as singles, our time can just as easily be consumed by much lesser activities. For those of us that hope to be married one day, how we spend our time now only sets the stage for how we might live in that kind of relationship, should that opportunity present itself.

My dad was formerly a financial planner and I remember hearing him talk to us as kids about the principle of generosity in the stewardship of our finances. If you do not practice generosity when you have little, you will not begin to give when you make more money. It is about the habits we create and choosing to live guided by them. No matter how much or how little we have, we learn to live out of those principles.

Living as a single is a unique season, with unique privileges and opportunities. I am no less responsible for how I spend my time than my sisters with their husbands and two babies. We are all accountable for how we respond to the invitations God has extended to us, for how we see our time and live into our calling.

The opportunities my eldest sister has because she is married and has kids is incredible. People interact with her everywhere she goes because her kids look like curly haired Cabbage Patch dolls dressed in fashionable denim. My brother-in-law is a pastor, and together with my sister, they help run a worship school in addition to their paid work hours. As a couple they teach and lead students to love Jesus more through lives of praise. Sometimes my sister and her husband, after a super long day of working balanced with child-care, baths, feedings, bedtime stories and clean up duties, sit down on their couch at night to begin prepping for one of the classes they are soon to teach. Their season of life is busy. And I fear if I were in their shoes, I would stop all my volunteer contributions, simply because I wanted 8 hours of sleep at night. But they see it as a joy to serve the church in this way. They are such role models for me (despite knowing I could not actually exist on the hours of sleep they routinely get!).

My other sister has two daughters. And while her husband works full days at a recruiting company downtown, she spends much of her time bringing joy to the lives of singles in their church, toting two babies in a stroller to visit neighbours, people whom she prays for and ministers to. She is often making meals for friends who have also had babies and is always inviting people into their home. I do not know many singles who spend their energy and time in such self-sacrificial ways.

We are all choosing how we spend our time. Whether married with kids, or single. My race is not yours, and yours is not mine.

Our lives look very different depending on what stage of life we are in.

But our God is constant. He is faithful to invite us, no matter our season of life, to give our YES *immediately* to him and to the adventures he has laid out for us.

Where has God called me to invest? Are there areas of my life where I squander the gifts he has given me, the opportunities he has put in front of me, simply because they are not the ones I thought I would have, or maybe want?

While single, I can pursue God's mission in ways that uniquely fit my calling, my gifts, my personality, and not worry that it hinders or pulls someone else away from what they are passionate about. Making decisions about how to live with a partner takes a lot more effort and planning. I have room to discover who God has made me to be, how he has wired me, and then run with the opportunities that embrace those gifts in ways that honour him.

The ways each of us will do this will differ, because we are different people.

For some, this might look like stepping up to volunteer at church. To find ways to plug in and serve the community, even if it is not in places where we are set up to meet potential partners.

It might look like saying "Yes" to opportunities we thought we would only want to do with a spouse. Going on a mission trip or considering a job that requires travel.

It could include using the creative giftings we have to make music or art, to collaborate on projects with other creatives.

It might simply look like gathering other singles together to form a more missional community that is less inwardly focused and more geared towards loving the neighbourhood and reaching out to coworkers.

We have not 'arrived' when we have reached marriage. And in the places where we might feel weak in our singleness, there the power of Christ is displayed for the world to see.

When we give a whole-hearted "Yes" to Jesus, and commit our time, our gifts and our capacity to him, he is more than able to multiply it beyond what anyone could ever imagine.

And rather than seeing singleness as a holding cell for a life that begins upon marriage, it is time to bust out and embrace the opportunities in front of us, *immediately*. To stop squandering our yeses, and to begin living.

The choice is mine.

And the choice is yours.

CHAPTER FOUR

Stop Shopping

"*You are what you eat.*" As a youth, I found this expression incredibly absurd. My childish love for eating dirt should have turned me into the world's whitest earthworm by middle school, if the saying has any truth to it! And yet upon watching the skin on my sister's fingers turn a literal orange after eating too many carrots in her first-year teaching, I swallowed my doubts and thanked the Lord that my childish habits had left me. Perhaps what I so unconsciously digested in my diet had greater metamorphosis power on my being then I had given it credit for.

Carrots and dirt aside, age and pop culture have their way of reinforcing the popular sayings we fail to grasp. And the truth in the pudding is pretty clear.

The more we consume, the more we become like what we consume. This is a problem when you live in an age of consumerism, like the one we find ourselves in today.

We have become a generation of shoppers. Shopping for happiness. Shopping for approval. Shopping for fame. Shopping for sex. Shopping for love.

We are bombarded by images of what our best lives should look like, what our best selves should look like, and all the things we need to get us there. The desire to be and have and become grows in us until we have little will power left, and the things we sought to consume are the very things that consume us.

We begin to forget what we were created for. We begin to forget how to create.

We are a generation of shoppers, with so many consumable options in front of us, we become better at critiquing than co-labouring.

We would rather visit churches and worship events, discussing how bad the music was and how unfriendly people were, than we would join the team of servers on Sunday morning, setting the stage for guests walking in. We would rather scroll through pages of Facebook feeds, analyzing people's posts and comments, liking and disliking them as we please, than walk over to our neighbours and start up a real conversation. It is easier to read the blogs about health, travel, and community projects than to put on our runners, fill up a travel pack, or fill out a volunteer application.

I am not immune to my culture.

I checked the screen time on my phone the other day and gasped. It was up a lot! Thankfully, the little nudge helped remind me to put my phone away and look at other things rather than Instagram, Facebook, WhatsApp and BBC news. No, I did not really need to know about the books, hikes, weddings, memes and cooked dishes everyone else was currently enjoying. I did have my own life going on. And I should probably focus more on what *that* included.

Some would say we are lucky to live in a day and age where we can live momentarily in the successes and adventures of someone else's life. It is thrilling and at times perplexing. We are so connected.

"He travelled there? She is with him? Their kid just pooped on the toilet for the first time?" As though I really care. I do not. Yet I do. And another little Instagram story has just lit up. And I really cannot sleep until I see what was posted. I am not addicted; I just need to open it in case it is important.

Shopping is how we live our lives. And we find humour in it. Why else have dating series exploded on TV? We enjoy watching people shop, even for love. As if *The Bachelorette* was not bad enough, we have now expanded our online options to include series like *Love Island* and *Dating Around*. Singles are thrown into experimental, sex-crazed environments and left to pick through the crowds, comparing conversations, bodies, and chemistry. We laugh at how ridiculous it is, and yet how many phones still wear the grease of fingerprints from swiping left and right over a bowl of chips with a blanket on the couch?

I am not against dating sites. I have had good friends use them and meet really great people through thoughtful searching and conversations. But looking for compatibility and sex appeal by screen are two different things. When we shop, we are looking for things that will fulfill our wants and needs. Our emotions and desires will not always motivate us towards wise decisions. And a shopping mindset leads us to value the best benefit to us rather than valuing a greater good or purpose.

In the past people used to shop for the important things in life together. Decisions were made in community. Purchases, plans for moving, jobs, even marriages. Now we make our decisions alone at our computers, filling our Amazon carts with more things we do not need, racking up purchase amounts we do not have. And we do this in isolation, consuming and consuming.

The problem is that this type of consumption does not fill us. *It leaves us craving for more.*

When my church did a New Year's fast together a year ago, our pastor asked us to choose things we wanted to put aside to spend more time with Jesus.

I asked, *"What is it Lord that you want me to fast from?"*

I hate fasting, the feeling of my gnawing stomach all day, growling at me as though I have abandoned the first cardinal rule of existence. So, I assumed I would hear: *"Fast, daughter, from food, good, sweet food."* Of course, he would ask me this.

But he didn't.

Okay, I did feel that I should fast from sweets, but this is something my sisters and I often do for the month of January to cleanse our systems from the month-long sugar blitz leading up to Christmas.

Sugary baking aside, I did not have a sense that I was to fast from food. Actually, the conviction I had was to fast from social media, and all the time I spent consuming. I was excited. This would hurt much less than giving up lasagna and my famous cheese stuffed crepes!

Gleefully, I deleted my Facebook and Instagram apps from my phone. I deactivated my accounts, and put a timer on my phone to limit how often I checked even email and text notifications in my day.

The first night, my phone sat on my bedside and it was eerily silent. I kept waiting for it to light up as per usual, but nothing happened. I was sure people were telling great stories and posting fabulous articles I should be reading. But how would I know? It was like a staring contest. I was waiting for my phone to blink, and it was waiting for my fingers to twitch. How long could I go without checking?

When the morning came, my hand automatically reached for the dead screen. But, alas, there was nothing to check. No one had messaged me stories while I slept. There were no mindless jokes, GIF's or updates about anyone's travel adventures. Or maybe there were. But I would not know.

Gone was my link to entertainment. I had no way to consume the highs and lows of everyone else's mornings around the globe. Strange to think that this could be a loss. Strange that it felt weird to start the day thinking only about my own day and the people I would see in it. Is this really how people used to live?

As the week went by the strange feeling of disconnectedness began to make me feel more connected to the people that were actually in my life. The ones I saw or called. The people on my bus whom I usually did not see because I was too busy messaging back and forth with friends about their dinner posts and weekend plans. I began to stop living in other people's worlds, and focus more on the one I was in, right then. I was not shopping through articles posted on web pages, choosing the ones I liked and disliked leaving a trail of expressive emojis to mark my approval ratings.

In a way, it was a reality check.

And because of it, I met Denise. Denise is the sweetest exchange student who lived one block from my house. One morning Denise happened to be waiting for the same 7AM #2 bus as myself, heading to downtown Vancouver for her English class. Phone tucked away, I noticed Denise shivering at the stop, and I asked her where she was from. Brazil. Of course. She had never seen snow and hoped it might snow this week, despite finding the temperature excruciatingly cold. She laughed at my 'sweater-coat' and wondered how I had not yet caught frostbite.

I discovered Denise shared my same bus route most days and only now, two months after her arrival, did I notice her. We became good friends. Denise started coming to my house for tea, and soon she met my roommates, then joined our games nights. Before long she was a regular visitor at our church. Denise became a really good friend - to think I might never have met her if I had been looking at my phone that morning immersed in the lives of others. I needed to be living mine!

There are many dangers of being a consumer. One is that we miss out on what we *already have,* or what is *right in front of us.* We have a life to live, and we might as well be awake to it!

Yet another danger of consumption is that through a shopper's mindset we begin to critique and compare. We begin to view other people in terms of what they can do for us. Whether in our friendships, our socializing at work or our dating relationships, we fixate on what we are getting out of the deal. We begin to grade our relationships. Do we stand to benefit from the relationship? Does it serve *my* purpose? And without even realizing it we can lose the meaning of connection as we begin to operate through a transactional mindset.

I see this so often in the kinds of communities we choose to interact in. Are the people we surround ourselves with all people we like? Do we only choose friends who have the means to bless us, encourage us, or act like us? Or do we allow ourselves to sit with those who are perhaps a bit more unique? People who might challenge our views, who might have a little less in common with us or who might not appear to enrich our lives as much as some of our other friends (although I've come to realize the opposite is more often true). It is far easier to pick and choose who we spend our time with based on what we want and desire, rather than learning to understand and empathize.

I brought up dating sites earlier because our dating lives can be no different. We say that marriage is a good thing. But is this because we actually believe in partnership? A give and take, sacrificial relationship, in which Christ is at the centre and the pursuit of his glory is the reason we desire to do life together? Do we embrace sacrifice as readily as we embrace the ideas we have of marriage? Or is the real reason because there is a need to fill a gap in our own lives? We feel alone and we want someone to make us feel less lonely? We want intimacy, a confidence boost, sexual release, children… is the criteria for how we choose a life partner based on what will get us those things in the easiest way possible? Are we looking for someone who will check the boxes?

I hear so often singles discuss the dating scene in our churches and frustratingly complain about the lack of godly men or women they know. They begin to compare the people they meet, shopping for partners by attending different churches, always with eyes to pick out the next 'maybe.' One of my former pastors used to call it the "lobby game." Post service pick-ups were almost like a trend.

But how dangerous that we might view one another in this light, seeing everyone as a potential, rather than a community of brothers and sisters! All too often we can find ourselves qualifying others on the basis of fulfilling our needs, and in doing so we miss out on genuine friendship, one that looks out for the best of one another. We commodify one another, rather than seek to value each other. What a loss this is to people in our world who could benefit from an incredible family of friends with a strong presence in our communities!

And as much as our shopping mentality keeps us analyzing our relationships with others, our tendency to consume and critique only puts us as losers in the very game we are playing. Because if we live as shoppers, surely we are under scrutiny too.

Consuming the world's image of what we should look like, what our lives should look like, can only lead us to see our own shortcomings. And so, we begin to project an image of ourselves that reflects what our culture says is valued. We fall prey to crafting the life that we have bought into. A life that the world celebrates, one that praises our beauty, our activities or our relationship status more than it does a depth of character or discipleship being formed in our lives. We show off a life that others might envy, while compromising on what brings us real joy. And as we do this, we compare ourselves, like clothes on a rack to what is being sold beside us.

How many likes do we have?

A friend of mine recently tried online dating. We debriefed her experience and she confided in me that her trial made her relationship status feel like a numbers game. For each profile uploaded into her account as a possible match she had to make a quick decision based on superficial facts whether or not to move forward with a conversation. The first reason for choosing to interact with someone no longer lay in the shared interests, passion, hobbies, or mutual community connections, but in a lowest common denominator: a photo. In addition, with disproportionately more women using this specific site than men, the pressure to feel that she had to profile herself in an attention-grabbing way just to snag the attention of someone scrolling through pages of photos felt ridiculous. It was a comparison game of winning and losing odds. Not having someone 'like' her photo back meant a sort of rejection - and this was by someone who had never even met her! She knew by the process she, herself had to follow, swiping through photos and analyzing captions, that she was being compared in the exact same manner. It was not very confidence boosting.

In the game of comparison and quick shopping we begin to see our faults and our failures as detrimental rather than opportunities for growth. We have consumed the idea that our lives need to look perfect.

And it motivates us to adopt inauthentic relationships.

This keeps us at a distance emotionally so that we cannot be truly known and loved by another.

And none of it measures up to the life we really want.

The more we become consumers of an ideal image of ourselves, agreeing with the brands, the comments, the advertisements... inevitably we find in ourselves a lack. We do not have enough. We are not enough.

If what I am consuming all too easily begins to narrate the story in my head, I should ask myself if I am willing to be controlled like this.

I will become like what I consume.

Our days will never be devoid of consumption, but we need to be aware of what we consume, how it is impacting us and learn to choose to fill ourselves with that which will bring life to our souls. Words of hope and truth. And we know where that is found.

When we shop and consume others, ideas, the picture our world gives us of the "ideal life," it is because we have begun operating out of a place of lack, rather than seeing our abundance. I need more clothes, I need more money, I need more attention, I need a spouse, I need children, I need friends who are like, or who have X, Y, or Z.

As singles is it easy to think that by not having a life partner we are in a place of deficit. We have a need that others do not, and therefore we operate out of a seeking spirit. We are always thirsting for more, for something that will fill that gap in our lives. We seek affirmation, self accomplishment, love from others. Sometimes through our value at work, our finances, and achievements. We consume every celebrated victory our world has deemed as such, in hopes that this other 'lack' in our lives will hurt a little less rather than acknowledge where that hurt truly stems from. And like a shopaholic, the highs we get when the world celebrates our 'medals' do not leave us more content, nor do they help us break away from our shopping habits. They leave us disappointed. What a faulty way to go through life.

We have an extravagant, abundant God who has poured himself out into us, filling our hearts with love, with joy and with peace. He is abundant in the ways he loves us and 'fills our love tanks' so to speak. If we will let him.

Our God is more than enough, and we do not need to look beyond him to find a life in which we are truly satisfied. This does not mean we will not accomplish great things in our lifetime or have deep loving relationships with others, but our worth and value will not stem from such pursuits or status. It will stem from knowing the depth of our worth which is found in him. It will stem out of a place of already knowing we are loved. *Full stop.*

I felt the Lord speaking to me about the extravagance of his love for me this past week. How I lack nothing in Him. In Psalm 37:4 it says: "*Delight yourself in the Lord, and he will GIVE you the desires of your heart.*"[1] I do not have to go looking for the things that will quench my desires, for the good things of God will be given to me.

This verse is so often taken out of context. People use it to justify any desires they might have, whether good or bad, and feel that God should listen to their requests. Entitlement is not a concept we are unfamiliar with.

But this verse speaks specifically to the things that we will desire *as* we delight ourselves in the Lord. Because the things we truly crave and that will satisfy us are not always the things we think we want. As we delight in Jesus our desires change, and the true cravings of our heart become manifest. *Those* yearnings he is more than happy to fulfill!

---

[1] Empasis added by author.

So, this past week I had the feeling to delight myself in the Lord, in the little things day to day that he wanted to show me. He demonstrated his love to me through his care for creation, the birds flying around the field out my window, through the ways he was present with friends of mine that had just experienced a death in the family, and in the way he brought me joy when my housing situation was less than ideal.

A few days later, however, I didn't really feel like satisfying myself in the Lord. I woke up feeling frustrated. Work was super intense - I run an employment program for women with high barriers. There are weeks when every conversation revolves around heart-breaking topics and mental health issues which seem to have no solution. That week had been particularly rough, and my energy level was lower than normal trying to support them through their journeys. My housing situation had fallen through, and I was dreading having to move again. This meant I would need to re-start with either new roommates, or seek out a place on my own and find all the furnishings for a new dwelling. Another friend of mine announced she was pregnant, which normally I would be super pumped about, but that day it reminded me of how different my season of life was from so many of my closest friends. It brought to mind how I would have yet another friend I would need to drive to and visit in her home, because she would need to be there by 7PM every night now for baby's sleep. It was silly, but I thought about it nonetheless.

I already felt a bit overwhelmed and as I looked through my Instagram thread I came across a photo of yet another friend who had recently gotten engaged. Her fiancé was hugging her tightly and the two of them were laughing on the beach. I heard a voice in my head say: *"You know, it would be kind of nice for someone else to take care of you for a change."*

Someone else.

An alarm sounded in my head. I knew this voice.

This voice of lies.

This voice that wanted me to believe that God did not understand my needs. A voice that declared God incapable of being enough for me, my manna for each day. It was the voice that whispered doubts about the race I was running. One that put questions in my heart about the love of the Father for me. *"If God truly loves you, would he not give you the desires of your heart, like he has for your friends?"*

Everything the Lord was trying to teach me that week came into opposition with the words I was hearing in my head.

So there I was. Facing an internal battle. Two voices, both fighting to be heard.

While God was wanting to fill my heart with satisfaction in him, the enemy was fighting to plant seeds of disillusionment and lack. He was using comparison to speak words of lies over me.

And suddenly I needed to choose which voice I was going to listen to.

I was grateful that the Holy Spirit brought this to my attention. So often I buy into the lies of the enemy without even realizing I have done so, without even realizing he is speaking. But here I was, knowing that I wanted to choose the voice of truth.

I reminded myself that what I needed to do in that moment was to delight myself in the Lord.

So, I did.

It was still quite early, and I had time before work to go for a walk, so I hopped in my car and drove out to a forested area near my house to just be with Jesus. To allow this voice of truth to speak to me.

It was a quiet morning, and I began to pray aloud as I strolled through the twisted path with overgrown shrubs. I asked God to teach me again how to delight myself in him. As I began speaking out words of praise, it was like he lifted my head. It was not instantaneous, but the longer I spent speaking out truths, praying out words of the Psalms back to the *one* who gave them to me, the more I felt a shift in my spirit. I began to hear songs running through my mind. Joyful songs. Songs of hope and of deliverance. Songs of praise.

Slowly, as I worshipped, my heart was no longer overwhelmed.

I decided to pick up a coffee on my way home. Normally I make just a plain dark roast coffee at home, but I decided to treat myself to a fun, flavoured sugary drink to sip on while I worked. I ordered the largest drink on the menu (even while doubting I could finish it) with extra shots of espresso and all the toppings. It felt extravagant even as I voiced my order through the drive through speakers.

When it was my turn to pick up and pay for my drink, I drove up to the window and smiled at the young girl with the headset and bandanna. She stretched out her arm passing my drink to me before I could give her my debit card, which seemed out of order. But when I held my card out to her, she flagged it away.

"Your drink has been paid for," she said, "the gentleman in the truck in front of you really wanted to buy it for you. He even had me write 'Happy Thursday' on the cup for you. It's nice the random times when I see strangers take care of someone else like that."

I was so surprised but thanked the barista and drove away smiling. It was just a coffee, but I knew it was more than that. I knew the Lord was wanting to show me in a tangible way what was on his heart. It was as though he was telling me: *"You are SO loved. I am taking care of you and I wanted you to know that this morning."*

What I had needed to consume that week was not the messages of my culture. It was not to compare my life, my relationship status, or my needs to those of anyone else. I needed to be aware that the enemy will always try to rob me of knowing where I find my purpose and my satisfaction. And he will use aspects of my culture, my desires and my struggles, to speak lies over me. But I needed to be caught up in the love of the Father. I needed to combat these lies with his promises. And that happened as I surrounded myself with his words and with worship.

My month of fasting from social media reminded me how easy it is to slip into a state of unawareness. When I become too caught up in consuming, I begin to crave what I do not have. I lose touch with what God has already put in front of me. The opportunities. The people. I do not need mindless recaps of other people's days and thoughts that leave me dissatisfied with my own. I do not need to shop through life, living a virtual reality show where I critique what others are doing and saying when they are not there to defend themselves. I do not need to operate out of a place of lack, as though my life is not as full or beautiful as someone else's who is in a romantic relationship.

I am loved.

My heart just needs at times to know this. And the way I know this is by filling myself with the truth of who I am in Christ, and the truth of who he says he is.

The more we consume, the more we become like what we are consuming.

I need real life. Imperfect life, that is unfiltered and ready to be explored. I need to stop consuming the superficial messages and images my culture says I must have and become, and I need to start creating.

In the absence of shopping, in the void of consuming, I find myself with a lot more space. Space to make memories, to meet people, to celebrate failures and victories and furthermore to see the potential of what God might want to do in and through me. How he might want to create with me a truly beautiful and fulfilling life. And suddenly I feel inspired!

CHAPTER FIVE

start creating

My sister is an incredible artist. Give her a paintbrush, a set of watercolours, and a pad of paper and within hours a display of dancers, flowers, or an intricate profile is ready to be framed and hung decoratively on a focal wall. I have tried my hand at painting. Never have I ever wanted to frame a picture I have drawn or painted. In my life. Never.

Except one time.

I tested out my art skills on an old roommate of mine in university. It took several hours to paint what I thought depicted an English cottage style landscape. It was detailed, full of vibrant spring colours, and was one of my better attempts at watercolour. I really got into the painting despite having no technique and using a pair of dishevelled brushes I had found under the kitchen sink. I was not going to waste money on what I knew would most likely turn into a sub-par creation.

Using an older antique frame I had stored in my room, I waited for the painting to dry before pressing it behind the glass cover. The vintage gold-speckled border really complimented the look I was going for. I mean, it was not amazing, but I didn't think it was as horrible as some of the other *"masterpieces"* I had attempted in the past.

I waited for my roommate, who was studying at the time to be a pediatric doctor, to return from class before showing off my artwork.

"I bought this today, at a garage sale," I lied to her, hoping to evoke an honest response.

And I got one.

"I wouldn't pay 25 cents for that painting," she said, "I hope you didn't waste your money."

I failed to mention that my roommate was from Germany and was known for her frankness of speech.

Thankfully I was not majoring in art, and neither was I offended. We had the best laugh after I told her the painting was mine and she apologized profusely, although somewhat insincerely, for her comment. As though I cared.

Despite knowing the painting was only a joke, the process of creating something and using my imagination was so life-giving I tried painting again the next week. And the next. It became a fun hobby, which I ended up using to make funny Christmas and birthday cards. I never framed any of my finished works. They really were not worth 25 cents. But I so enjoyed attempting to bring shape, colour and size to a thought or idea that was rolling around in my head. It was fun to actualize what I thought could be really beautiful, whether it turned out the way I wanted it to or not. At least I tried. And perhaps that is the beauty of creating.

When we operate out of a state of consuming, we lose the art of creating. And this is a huge loss, not only to us, but to others. We were made to create. To see the world and the people in it with eyes of possibility and potential. To help bring about transformation. To be culture changers. To cultivate home, purpose and identity in our own lives, and then in community around us. Lives that are brimming and breathing with passion. Because all of this started somewhere. With someone.

We are co-creators with Christ, the one who created us. And with the *mind* of Christ *in* us, we can ask the Holy Spirit to inspire us to live lives that reflect his character to create with him. There is an interplay between the shaping of what happens in and through us, and our maker shows us how this is done. Not only are we the clay, being molded and formed hopefully more and more into the likeness of Christ, there are also things in our lives that we are invited to help shape and create.

And as we say yes to this, we have the joy of watching things grow and flourish and take form. We do not simply watch as life happens to us, but with our lives we engage with the tools, gifts and opportunities God gives us: A lifestyle conducive to the Spirit's moving. It is then that we begin to see what *can happen* during our lifetime. We have the opportunity to dream!

In the first chapter, "If," I wrote about the shift from seeing a projected life as one which *will* get married to one which *might*. WHEN becomes IF. There is so much room to dream with Jesus when we stop living out of a closed framework for how our lives are supposed to look. We need to be receptive to whatever plans our Father has for us. And I would dare us to go a step further that we might even embrace the potential that they bring.

And If I Don't: Reimagining the Single Life

A teacher friend of mine plays a game with her high school students called "If-Then". She reads to them a possibility and allows them to respond.

Teacher: "If I won a million dollars…" Student: "Then I would buy a boat and sail to Hawaii on my birthday!"

Teacher: "If I could never die…" Student: "Then I would try skydiving, and river rafting and bungee jumping…!!"

Teacher: "If I could travel backwards in time…" Student: "Then I would have lunch with Abraham Lincoln and Elvis Presley and…!!!"

It is interesting how the youth completely light up at the thought of what they can do when multiple options are given to them. Dreaming about potentials for their lives brings them so much joy and they have no problem coming up with creative ways of living them out.

So why is it that dreaming about a life outside of marriage so often does not bring us the same joy and creativity? Should it?

Self: "If I don't get married…"

Then what?

Silence.

It feels risky to think of living our lives outside of preconceived notions we have grown up with. In some ways it is like our comfort zone. We are comfortable living in a way where certain actions lead to certain future predictions and desires. (As though we can truly control them.) When you take a risk, you can never know what an outcome will be. Most often, we find ourselves drawn to focus on those that are negative.

It might feel risky to think of a life in which you do not get married. What that will look like is unknown. That sort of life does not involve many of the natural progressions that our married friends anticipate. A season of engagement, honeymooning, pregnancy, parenting and eventually grandparenting etc. (A sort of life which seems to have a built in clock of seasons.) And in the void of all these things, there is a whole life to figure out. An unknown life, with possibility, but a new paradigm. It is a risk. And it plays with our fears. It does not always invoke a joy filled response.

Again, I have to ask: "Should it?"

Singleness is described in Scripture as a gift. And often when we talk about singleness being a gift, we think of people who have really embraced this aspect of their life. "So-and-so, *must* have the gift of singleness, they really live it out well." We assume that they have been given a specific call to singleness and therefore their joy in living as a single just flows out of this place. Unlike the rest of the singles who are suffering in loneliness…

I have personally been asked many times if I have this calling, this gift of singleness. Most likely this is because I highly esteem singleness and speak well of the opportunities that come with being single. But surprisingly enough, my answer to those who ask me about having this gift is not what they expect to hear.

To be completely honest, I would love to get married and have a family.

Yes, I have the gift of singleness. But I believe everyone who is single does. While it might not be the gift we would have chosen for ourselves, it is something God has entrusted to us for right now, and for an unknown amount of time.

Very often, we do not choose the gifts we are given, just as we do not choose so many aspects of the lives we live. But if the gift giver is good, I must then believe that the gift is good also. Therefore it is worthy of me unpacking, exploring, and watching what comes to fruition through its use.

There are many things about how God works that I cannot understand. But he is faithful and I do know, even from my own life story thus far, that I can trust him. God is creative in how he writes our stories. He is not limited or bound to a certain narrative. It is I who too often minimize his ability to write my story, or that of a colleague's or family member or friend, in the way that I deem best.

In the same way, we see the word joy used in Scripture in so many kinds of circumstances. And not always in the ones we would expect. I remember being shocked when I read the words in Hebrews 12:2 which, speaking about Jesus, says who: *"for the joy that was set before him endured the cross."* How could anyone find joy in such a painful and excruciating experience? And what about when James writes: *"Count it all joy, my brothers, when you meet trials of various kinds."*[1] The joy being described in these passages is not speaking about an initial outcome that any of us would choose, but it is speaking about a joy that is related to a greater purpose, a greater good connected to each situation.

Singleness is not the worst thing that can happen to someone. Yet sometimes we treat it like it is a curse that has ruined our lives. I want to challenge us, no matter how we feel about our singleness, to count it a joy. Because there is joy to be found in singleness *if* we see the purpose in it. *If* we dream about

---

1 James 1:2

what that could actually mean. Choosing to embrace the gift of singleness that I find myself entrusted with means I need to start letting go of control.

Can I still hope for marriage? I have said this a few times now, but the answer is YES. Absolutely. But my hope to be married one day does not mean I pursue it as the ultimate answer to a desire I have. Marriage is not the final solution to my loneliness. But until I let go thinking that it is, I will try to manipulate my story, or I will live in dissatisfaction rather than in gratitude and wonder at how God might be creatively at work. I will miss the opportunity to join him.

Adventuring with Jesus will always include joy and heartache. It is a life of surrender that will ask me to submit, to follow the call of my Saviour. Sometimes this will be really hard. But through submission to God's plan for our lives, we can begin to allow his dreams to give us joy. We can come alive with an unimagined life because the author of our stories is so creative!

This, again, might mean we need to be willing to risk, because creating a life with God where we trust in an unknown outcome regarding our singleness means we must also embrace a lot of questions that we might not yet have answers to. Below are just a few of the questions we might be asking ourselves:

"What if my life will be lonely down the road as a single?"

"Will I always be the odd one out in my friend circles?"

"Will I look back and regret not having had a family?"

These are not small questions.

But, if we believe that God desires to love us, to fill us and even to use us in his redemptive plan for the world, then I have to wonder how he might want to use our singleness to answer the very questions we ask of ourselves. To bring purpose and joy in our season of life.

When I ask **whether my life might be lonely down the road**, I am tapping into a big problem, one that my generation (and world) is struggling with in immeasurable ways. Why was the world's first ever Loneliness Minister appointed in the United Kingdom in 2018 to tackle what was named as the country's greatest current health challenge?[2] Loneliness is a real issue. And for many singles, considering a life void of a consistent life partner feels daunting. But what are some unique ways as a single that God might want to meet me in my loneliness and transform that into a richness of relationship with him? I have so much time in my singleness to invest in my relationship with God. Can I pursue intimacy with him in the unique ways available to me as a single? Can I learn to embrace the unhurried mornings and evenings to sit on the beach and soak in the presence of God? What about time steeped in Scripture because I am not frantic to get a carload of kids to school? I have more space to read and study than I would as a married person, especially one with children.

Furthermore, as I seek contentment in the depth of friendship with my creator, how might I be able to invite others to experience that friendship and partnership together? Am I willing to create with the Father a sort of living that uses my own struggles as a place to welcome others in? Do I even know how many singles

---

2   "PM Launches Government's First Loneliness Strategy." *Government of United Kingdom*. 2018. Web Press Release.

in the spaces around me are struggling with that same question of loneliness? Maybe God planted me beside one of them as an answer to their prayer. God is at work in our lives because he loves us even if this means he works through a challenging aspect of our lives that we have not sought. Using something like loneliness to draw us closer to him is an underestimated gift. And when he brings change into our lives it should never stop there, but should flow out into the world that we might reflect and point others to know and be loved by him too.

When I ask myself if **I will always be the odd one out** in my friend circles, have I considered that the uniqueness of my situation might be both a blessing to others and to my own journey? How might it help make me more attentive to those around me who feel like they are misfits for other reasons? Do I recognize the ways that people coming into our churches might feel out of place like I sometimes do at dinner parties with all married friends? Does my heart have more compassion for someone who cannot get pregnant when all their friends are, or when a friend shares a struggle that might not be visible to anyone else? How might the company of these persons enhance my own understanding of the richness of the church?

When I ask myself if one day **I will look back and regret not having had a family,** I have to ask myself how willing I am to fully embrace the family of God. Can I truly see family *redefined by Jesus* as those who do the will of the Father? Would the spiritual children that might come as fruit from a life well lived for Jesus reflect this? Would I rejoice as much over this kind of family as I would a biological baby? Could I trust a creative loving Father that he might find other ways for me to experience family, and enjoy the company of mothers, aunties, cousins, and brothers that have no blood relation to me, but for whom I have more than enough space for in my life? To experience love from others. To be family to some who have perhaps struggled to know love amongst their own?

Our greatest struggles often become the places where the gospel most transforms us.

It happens in the ways we least expect it.

At the core, releasing myself to embrace these potentials means I must let go of the fear I have when I give up control.

Because what if God's best plan for me was to remain single?

What if I truly embraced his call and took him at his word when he said that he was good, and that his plans for me were not just second best, but his best? Would I find joy and purpose? Would I begin to see the potential of what we might create together?

How might the ways I spend discerning the years ahead shift in light of this view? And how can I walk a tightrope, holding to these promises while still believing that *perhaps* marriage might be in his plans?

I do not believe that we must give up hoping for marriage in order to embrace or value singleness. I do not believe in a zero-sum game. There are no losers and winners. But what does it look like to create a life when all I know right now is that I am single?

As someone who still desires marriage, I have given thought to how this looks in my own life. How might I think outside the box, or dream about the future, not knowing if marriage will ever happen? What kind of life would Jesus and I create together?

I believe there are so many opportunities in front of me: several of which I have already tested out. I have taken jobs that I probably would not have accepted if I were in a long-term relationship. Jobs that have required a lot of commitment, and which have had me travelling for significant amounts of time. Some of these jobs have been incredible. Life changing. They have expanded my world views, grown my skills, and brought rich friendships into my life.

Looking forward, I have been pondering and praying about whether one day I might either foster or adopt. I have always desired to be a mom, and should that opportunity never actualize, I still have a lot of love to give to a child that could otherwise be waiting for someone to take them in. Now would that not be an adventure?

I have also decided, after talking to a very wise mentor, that every year or so I will bring my plans and hopes before the Lord and ask of him: "Is this still the direction you want me to head in, or is there something in the way I am living or the pursuits of my life that you want to see change?" Of course, I could do this with a spouse, but as I have already mentioned I have an unusual freedom as a single to ask God how he might want to use my specific gifts and calling to serve him, without wondering if it might hinder or detract a partner from their call.

I can also take risks right now as a single that will not have an impact on my spouse, or the wellbeing of my children should things not pan out the way I expect them to.

I do not need a husband and children to have a life that looks beautiful and even appealing. I need Christ, his vision, his colourful plan for my life to be splashed all over the canvas. And this is exciting!

I refuse to be sidetracked by a single view of beauty when the diversity of the seasons of our lives are perhaps one of the most incredible reflections of who our God is. A creator, a storyteller, a painter. A God that purposes each part of the body of Christ to play a role in his story.

Creativity is at the center of who God is. And I am so glad that I can trust him when he invites me to create a life with him.

CHAPTER SIX

deliberate

I typed in "how to untap creativity" into the Google search engine. Not surprisingly, the first things that appeared were directives like: *"Get uncomfortable, be present, embrace the new,"* words that directly correlated to what we discussed in the previous chapter. But as I continued to read, I noticed that articles featuring creativity often emphasized how creativity was a process, one that was learned and practiced. Artists who have produced beautiful masterpieces for us to enjoy were deliberate in their planning, even though the stages of their processes often seemed messy to the outsider. Deliberately following a plan led to a creative work of something truly admirable.

Process, and belief that something beautiful would emerge, was at the center.

God is deliberate in his plans for our lives and I believe that he is calling us as singles to be deliberate in how we live ours. To create a life with him that is based on a strong foundation. One that is anchored in truth so that even when we do not recognize the beauty of what he is creating in, through and with us right now, we trust it will be.

Cultivating a life of joyful adventure and purpose stems from a life that is rooted first in Christ. It is from this rootedness that if we are to ask ourselves: *"If I don't get married?"* What pours out are fruits of the Spirit: love, joy, peace, patience... no matter where we find ourselves in life.

Jeremiah 17:7-8 says *"Blessed is the man who trusts in the Lord, whose trust is the Lord. He is like a tree planted by water, that sends out its roots by the stream, and does not fear when heat comes, for its leaves remain green, and is not anxious in the year of drought, for it does not cease to bear fruit."*

A healthy tree is one that is planted: it has roots. It is connected to the *one* that fills it with joy and creativity and overflow. If singleness feels like a desert time for you because marriage has always been the dream, then there is no better time to dig deep. One of the ways I have found my roots is by having **spiritual rhythms** and **healthy habits,** and being deliberate about creating a lifestyle which includes them. Because if our practices end up shaping us, I sure hope I am intentional about the ones I am including in my life!

Having roots is like setting up the canvas on which one can paint. It is the foundation from which a piece of creativity emerges.

SPIRITUAL RHYTHMS:

But what are rhythms anyway?

I took drum lessons for a few months somewhere in my mid-twenties. I was actually decent at it, or so my drum teacher said (that could have been because he was dating my sister). But I did not stick it out too long (that could have been because he and my sister broke up). In any case, I learned a lot from my instructor, including the importance of a steady cadence, which allowed frills and cymbals and high hats not to be mere noise distractions. The consistent beat that I needed to find, either with the bass drum or the high hat, allowed my beginner attempts to find a pace; a pattern to anchor the song with. At times I lost the steady pulse and everything else fell to shambles. I was simply making a ruckus, and an ugly one at that! Although my mistakes never really bothered me, I am pretty sure it had the neighbours shaking their heads. Thankfully, my lessons were always at my drum teacher's house, and I maintained my dignity when pulling up to my own.

Without the consistency of the rhythms which guide our lives, life can feel chaotic. It can feel like we are making a lot of noise trying to hit the things we are supposed to. My job might be the high hat. My friendships, the snare. My family, the kick drum. And my dating life? Definitely the cymbals!

There is a lot of noise going on and little direction. Somehow it is all supposed to work together.

And then there is the most important question: "Where is God in the mix?"

Our lives need to include rhythms that will keep us grounded. Spiritual rhythms of *scripture, prayer, solitude, silence, praise* and *sabbath*. Practices that will keep us in sync with the flow our lives are supposed to follow. Not a flow that our culture says we should head towards, but one which draws us back to what is important. To the *one* at the center. To where our roots grow.

These rhythms are not new, nor has the discussion of their importance been ignored. But part of the reason there are so many books and podcasts popping up these days around the importance of spiritual rhythms is because we are not very good at practicing them.

We know they matter, but we are far too busy to practice them with intentionality.

As singles, we must choose what is filling our minds and our hearts. If we do not, our world will do it for us, and it will most likely emphasize the things we don't have. Being anchored in the truth of our identity as daughters and sons of God trumps any label that the world could put on us, or on the races we are running. Single. Alone. Rejected. Second Best.

Scripture: Spiritual rhythms help us know God and know who we are because of him. Nothing reminds me more of God's good plan for my life then his words, Scripture, which guide me along the best paths for my life. And sometimes we really need to be reassured of this. When our plans for marriage fall through, and we never thought about a different kind of life, Psalm 119:105 says *"Your word is a lamp to my feet and a light to my path."* He has not left any one of us without a plan.

Prayer: We know God through his word just as we know him through prayer. Communication with the Father not only reminds us that we are not alone, but shapes our perception of the world and the decisions we are making. Prayer reminds us of our need for God, greater than our need for anything else. It is greater than our work successes, or the need to keep our perfect image together. It is greater than our need for a life partner. And it brings us back to a place of surrender, confession, repentance and refills us with the thoughts and mind of Christ. Oh, I need this daily. I so need to admit that I am not the one in control.

That I do not have all the answers. That as much as I might want something, or someone, I want him more.

Solitude: Another rhythm I have been trying to carve into my life for quite some time now is solitude. Now, as a single, one would think that solitude should already be a thing. Perhaps, for some it is, however I have found this is something I have to fight for. I have spoken to many singles who agree that it is tempting to fill our schedules full of social things, so as not to feel alone in our singleness. But it becomes difficult then to embrace the moments where this might be a great gift to our own growth and development as followers of Jesus. Just as you cannot only date someone in a group setting, our relationship with Jesus cannot develop to the same depth if we only spend time with him in church gatherings or bible studies. The intimacy our souls crave is found in being alone with the Lord, and this is something we must learn to prioritize.

I love the quote from Jon Thompson in his book *Convergence:*

"Solitude is not the rejection of human company but recognition of the limits of human company. We need others, but not more than we need God."[1]

We were built for this kind of intimacy and connection with the Father, and we need to create space for this to grow. How many married friends of mine are new parents and long just to have a fraction of the solitude my schedule permits me to have? And yet, I seem to take it for granted. I have loved my moments with Jesus hiking on a quiet trail or sitting on my favorite couch

---

1 Thompson, Jon. *Convergence: Why Jesus Needs to be More Than Our Lord and Saviour to Thrive in a Post-Christian World.* Sanctus Church. Print. 2018.

with a cup of coffee. It is a special phase of life to have the amount of time I do to soak in God's presence!

Silence: Just as I must fight to be alone with God, I must be deliberate in seeking silence amidst my busy distracted mind if I truly wish to hear him speak. In the quiet we know him. To have ears to hear should he want to speak. A friend of mine recently shared that silence is a spiritual rhythm that scared her for years. As someone who was not yet married, she was always afraid of what God might say if she stopped to listen. That she was to break up with her boyfriend who was not a believer, or that she was to stay single her whole life. But the day she decided to actually listen, she said all she heard were words of affirmation. That she was loved, and that she was not alone. She cried for hours, and it began a change in her relationship with God.

Praise: Another rhythm that can shift our understanding of God is praise. Something happens in our spirit when we agree with the truth that God is good, that he is faithful, and that he is worthy. Suddenly we find ourselves enamoured by God's goodness and faithfulness, no matter the situation we find ourselves in. Single. Married. Divorced. Widowed. God is still good. Praising God helps us to lift our eyes and hearts above the concerns and weight of what we cannot always understand about our life circumstances.

I personally love engaging in a variety of activities which help redirect my praise towards God. Worshipping through song, meditating on God's word, studying Scripture etc. I find that in different seasons the ways I connect with him vary just as my relationship with the Lord never needs to be static.

Sabbath: I also believe that taking time to sabbath is so important to incorporate into our rhythms of life. Sabbath is a day of rest in our week. Not just a day to 'check out' and drown ourselves in mindless activities, but to be present and enjoy our relationship with God, with creation and with others. When we practice sabbath, we engage in a counter cultural movement, calm in contrast to hustle. As singles, it is easy to pack our weekends full, to maximize our 'office-free' days, running errands and being in too many places at once. But our spirits need to be reminded of the patterns of rest which God calls us to. That at the start and end of each week we begin and end with the rest which is found in him and in his community.

The spiritual rhythms that we are called to engage in are for our benefit, and for the benefit of the community around us. I think it is important, however, to remember that these are not a list of rules to be followed. A happy single life is not the product of following a handbook. Just like jazz band members listen to one another, shifting their solos and riffs to accommodate the flow which keeps the song moving along, the spiritual rhythms in our life are not about rules and duty but rather delight and movement towards Christ. There are times when the rhythms we engage in are sobering. And that is okay. There are seasons when God might seem distant, and the choice to continue engaging in the pursuit of him might feel overwhelming. But they are important because we know they will keep us rooted in the source of what brings hope and joy into our lives.

Time abiding in Christ can only bear fruits of the Spirit in our lives. And I do have to say that some of my greatest moments of laughter have come straight out of my times of solitude and silence, prayer and reading Scripture, as the breath of God fills me with purpose, delight in him, and with deep, deep joy.

HEALTHY HABITS

So what else are we invited to deliberately cultivate in our lives? Spiritual rhythms are just one aspect of living a wholehearted, healthy life, and as beings with both physical and emotional desires, we are also invited to create and practice healthy habits which can help us understand how to value and thrive in the lives we have been given as singles. The habits we seek to incorporate into our lifestyles might not only enrich our own journeys, but they can also have a profound impact on people around us. We are called to be culture shifters. And one way we do this is through the habits we live out of, healthy habits of *time, finances, self-care,* and *boundaries.*

One of the habits that I want to touch on is the practice of generosity. The generosity of our time and our finances.

Time: For those of us who are not married, there are ways we might experience specific opportunities to be generous because we are single. For one we have the opportunity to practice the generosity of our time. And the use of our time conveys so much about what we value.

As a single, I simply do not have the same sort of time constraints that my married friends do, especially those with children. But as a single I do have to ask myself then if the time I have is mine to spend, or if I am using it in ways that reflect the heart and mission of Jesus? Do I create habits that allow me to use my time in Jesus centered ways? Is my life one that is connected to the rhythms of others? Is it interruptible? Are my hours planned around my own joy or are they held openly that they might bless others and even be multiplied?

In 1 Corinthians 7 Paul calls those who are not married to embrace the gift of time and to use it charitably. To see the opportunities available to singles, simply because their focus is not centered around their home life. There is room to fully give their thoughts and time to whatever the Lord would call them to. And if we truly understand the mission and call of Christ, we cannot help but be enraptured by what we are called to. That he would choose to use us, is still a mystery to me!

One way I personally have felt called to be generous with my time is through my mobility as a single. It is easier for me, in my stage of life to physically go to other people. I do not always need to be the one going, but on occasion this can be a huge blessing to someone who does not have the ability or capacity to do so. The way this has played out has taken on different forms in different chapters of my life. Right now, it looks like going across town. There are days when driving to visit with a friend who has just had a baby, taking a newcomer friend to see the doctor, or dropping off groceries might be the best use of my time. At other times in my life, my going has included travelling globally. Some very memorable experiences in my life have involved implementing creative social projects around the world which bring people together and create spaces for them to be known in community.

When I was in my late twenties, a door opened up for me to join a team, which was putting together youth camps in the Middle East. What seemed like a crazy idea became a concrete plan. Before I knew it, I ended up joining a group of 20 North Americans helping to facilitate peace camps in Turkey and Iraq. The camps brought together young adults from refugee camps and settlement areas with host country participants, to discuss what it meant to embody peaceful leadership. Five years have passed since I said "Yes" to this invitation, and I do not think my life, nor my views of the world will ever be the same.

For three repeating summers we sat around circular tables in a room of 40-110 young adults, listening to each other's stories, crying with one another, dancing and sharing about our cultures. I remember sitting across from a young Yazidi refugee in Northern Iraq at one of these camps. Her people had lived through a horrendous genocide and the only contact they'd had with foreigners was when they were filmed so the news of their plight could be broadcast to viewers in North America. Now having people travel across the world just to spend time with them, she said, was the best gift they could have received. To think that strangers would care enough to travel that far just to be with them!

My friend's comment was such a wakeup call for me. The chance to be a part of these peace camps had at first sounded like such a huge time commitment. It meant travelling to places that were not as comfortable as where I was living in Europe at the time. It meant hours of waiting for visas, Skype calls at 3AM because of time differences, and money spent on tickets and gifts. And yet, I sit here today a changed person because of all that I have received through the process. My flexible schedule, life stage, and ability to connect with other young single people was one of the greatest gifts God could have given me in that season of my life.

Currently, I am living back in North America. My life has been no less enriched by the open doors I have had to work with women of the lower income sector in my city, or by helping to start up events like Alpha for young people in my own local context. These opportunities are using my joy to be with people, to create spaces and to build connections. This is what I was created for. This is how I have been called to create. And I want to be *deliberate in using my time* in ways that bring God glory.

Now I know that not everyone shares the same passions as I do, to travel, to create community projects etc. But each of us, whether married or single has unique gifts to use for the Kingdom and when we make space and allow the Spirit to creatively lead us in how we use our time, we will experience riches far greater than we could if we hoarded them for ourselves.

I will admit, there are many times I get this wrong. It is all too easy to live for the weekends, and after all… the mountains are always calling me! I regularly have to check my heart as I look at my agenda, to see if I have paused to ask the Lord how he might want me to spend the hours of my week. Not that I shouldn't have days of refreshment and sabbath, but I shouldn't stop only at that. Incredible opportunities exist all around me, and if I seek the Father's heart he will show me which ones align with who I was created to be.

Finances: Just as we have been called to create habits of generosity with our time and mobility as singles, I also believe our finances should reflect a lifestyle that is centered around Kingdom goals. Money is addressed so many times in Scripture and how we spend our money matters to Jesus. As singles we have opportunities to get creative with our budgets, to bless others and to steward the finances God has given us for his purposes. As singles, our finances might not be as tied up as some of our married friends supporting children. Can I get inventive in the ways I might be called to spend? Would I even dare ask other singles to join me in my giving?

Self-Care: I also want to touch on the habit of self-care, or caring for our physical bodies, which in a sense is a generosity towards ourselves. We have a choice in how we care for our bodies. We can run them ragged on little sleep, a poor diet, and moderate to no exercise, or we can fuel them with nutrients, strength training and find balance between rest, work, and play. Our culture emphasizes too strongly the image that our physical bodies need to take on, especially for singles, who fall prey to believing that *this* is what will help attract a partner. And whether or not that is true, health is not a matter of mere image. It is important to find a place of personal health from which you can thrive and function. It is surprising how finding ways to challenge and stretch yourself physically enables you to feel more prepared for opportunities that open up, simply because your health is more stable than it would otherwise be.

Sometimes as singles we need a little motivation to find the right balance. We need friends to spur us on, maybe a person to text us an hour before the fitness class starts, or to remind us to go to bed a little earlier in the week. Practicing a healthy lifestyle with regards to food and exercise does not have to be something we do alone. And as we learn to live into empowering habits, we have the opportunity to invite others to join us.

Boundaries: The last habit I want to touch on is that of creating good boundaries, as this is foundational in the lifestyles we are forming. As singles, and especially if you live alone, there is less of a built-in accountability structure to help navigate what our sabbath looks like, what we commit our time to, and where we spend our finances and passion. Creating boundaries helps free us to pursue the things the Spirit is leading us towards. I personally have found that inviting community to speak into certain areas of my life has helped me to maintain parameters around questionable boundaries I might have. The more I examine my own boundaries, and then invite trusted individuals to help keep me accountable to them, the more I find a greater freedom.

For each of us, those boundaries and conversations of accountability will look different depending on where or to what we are most inclined to give ourselves. If we struggle in areas of finance, opening our lives to allow community to speak into our purchasing and saving habits can help us become better stewards of what we have been entrusted with. Otherwise, who sees what we spend our money on? As singles we don't have a joint bank account!

And finances are just one example. What about the dating life of a single? I dare say we need better boundaries in place, in the culture we live in, if we are to live with purpose and vision in how we date. The pressure of *when* you should get married tends to push us either towards serial dating or relationship compromises.

I recently watched a show on Netflix called *Indian Matchmaking*. Actually, I watched the first three episodes of the show with my dad, and it was hilarious. It made me think about the way our culture has shifted in its orientation from a *communal* to *individual* dating mindset. In traditional Indian culture arranged marriages were, and are still considered, a viable option for finding a spouse. And the process involves the whole family.

The show had my dad and I in stitches as we watched awkward first encounters of potential couples taking place in family homes where grandparents, parents and even siblings were included in the occasion. The doorbell rings and the invited *potential* walks into a circle of 3-8 people who are analyzing their conversation, compatibility, posture etc. Talk about pressure!

And yet, there was a beautiful sense of the value of community in helping the singles make good dating choices. While at times the pressure of the community was a little intense, in our Western individualized culture we still have a lot to learn about this process, and the inclusion of community in the ways we choose a spouse, as well as in the boundaries we set for ourselves in dating.

Other boundaries include one's practices of sexual purity (which we will discuss more in the next chapter) and community itself.

I love community and I am passionate about creating community, but I realize that as singles, we often have one of two leanings. Either we *over-indulge* in community or we *isolate*. Both can be dangerous. We need to realize that we are strong, capable individuals, able to rely on the Father to help us make choices and hard decisions. We also need community, to journey with us and to speak into our lives. But sometimes we can push too far into one or the other. Like a pendulum, it is easy to swing towards or away from community as a coping mechanism. No, we do not need to saturate ourselves in community as a medication, to numb the aloneness that we might sometimes feel. It is actually okay to lean into an understanding that we have an ache for companionship. It reminds us of our need for God. On the other hand, we do not have to fall into traps of isolation. Life in community is hard and when we are hurt or afraid of rejection the easier path can be to withdraw. We need to practice healthy habits that will return to us.

Developing boundaries in our lives is important because without them unhealthy habits can lead us to pursue things other than those which draw us closer to Christ. And when this happens, shame can so easily creep in. We stop doing the things we know are best, and we give in to practices that leave us wounded, vulnerable and tired. We cannot even think about the life and passions we have to create with. We return to consuming. We begin believing lies, buying into our culture, ingesting the wrong messages, and the enemy knows how easy it is for us to swallow this - hook line and sinker. The more he can get us alone, the more we are his targets. We need to create spaces of accountability, where we can check in with others about how we are doing in upholding the boundaries we have set up, not just to say we are good, but to walk in greater freedom as sons and daughters.

As we begin to live out of healthy habits and foundations, we are following Christ's lead in our lives. Living with purpose. Deliberate about the ways we engage in his world. Again, we are setting the stage for what he can and might want to do in and through our lives.

In the final chapter, I will talk about how life in a community of believers is so vital to our health and purpose as singles.

For now, I will simply say that in the ways we determine to live our lives with purpose, through healthy spiritual disciplines and habits, we are creating spaces where we can invite others to join us, to experience healthy living in community. As we invite people in to share in our lives, what we are co-creating with Christ will be multiplied and impactful. Generosity breeds generosity. Healthy boundaries set an example for others. Sometimes it takes going first. Creating something that others can be invited into. A way of life. Opportunity. When the generation around us says, "we will shop through this life," can we offer a different option?

This last year, I have had the beautiful opportunity to experience this kind of living in two different ways. In one example, *I had the opportunity to invite*. And in the other, *I was invited in*. In both examples, the beautiful mesh of healthy habits and creative invitation together enriched my life in such a positive way.

The first example:

Over a year ago, my sister and I discussed a similar struggle we had. We wanted to be more intentional with several friends in our community. To better know how to encourage and love them and to be Christ's hands and feet in practical ways. As a mom of two, my sister did not have a million extra hours to spend visiting with each friend she loved. As a single, I wanted to start something to invite my community into, but like for most singles, I found it hard to always start things alone.

We decided to deliberately spend time in prayer, seeking the Father's heart for the wonderful women he had placed in our lives. We waited on the Lord, and discussed how we felt him speak to us. And somewhere amid our discussions, he gave us a truly beautiful idea: to start a book club. It was a way we could join together and consistently show up for our friends. We could be deliberate with our time and energy to bring people together and create space for meaningful conversation.

Now a book club might not sound like the world's most creative idea, but I truly believe it stemmed from our times of prayer and listening. It became one of the highlights of my entire year, and several of our friends mentioned they felt the same way.

Book club became the once a month gathering where we divulged our different literary findings over a cracker and cheese charcuterie board. It was an excuse to show up for each other and to be in one another's homes. Each month we visited a different club member's house. When it was someone's turn to host, they would choose the book and then lead the discussion questions.

We were part way through the year of book club when COVID-19 broke out. And honestly, with so many of us being stuck at home during long winter months, the opportunity to continue meeting over Zoom was amazing. Even though we were gathering by screen we continued to maintain a sense of connection and something to look forward to. There was no way my sister or I could have planned for that, but God knew and he led us to start something that became life-giving during one of the most uniquely challenging seasons any of us had ever lived through.

The second example:

In recent months a younger church friend of mine confided in me that he was struggling to read Scripture. That he was always lost as to where to start reading, how to understand the texts and in all the confusion, he was tempted to give up reading it all together. I encouraged him not to quit, but to press on, as I knew how enriching it was to know God daily through his words. At the same time, I had recently finished a scripture study I was personally tracking with, and I wasn't really sure where to pick up again myself. I wanted to offer my friend something, but I didn't have the energy to meet with him on a regular basis, as I was feeling overly committed at church and my days were quite full of other obligations. But it seemed that we could both benefit from some kind of structured approach.

Shortly after our discussion, another single friend from church reached out to a group of us, inviting us to join him on a bible study app. The idea was to follow a yearly bible reading plan, which allowed us to track with one another and share comments on what God was speaking to us that day from our readings. It was so simple, it was perfect!

Amazingly the online group became an incredible source of encouragement in my journey of reading Scripture. I loved seeing each day in the comment section what my friends were hearing from God, to feel like I was a part of a group on a connected spiritual journey, instead of on my own. It was also a blessing to know that my younger church friend was benefitting from the interpretations of Scripture others were commenting on.

A little idea sparked an awesome way for several of us singles in the church to feel more connected. To continue practicing a spiritual rhythm that was foundational in our walks with God. And I was thankful to my friend, who by a simple text, invited me in.

So often as singles we wait to be invited in. To be given a place at the table. While this is beautiful, it won't always happen. There are times when it is our turn as singles to invite others in. To realize that we have something to offer, community to create, ideas to contribute for the good of a bigger group. We do not always have to wait for someone else to go first.

As we become people who have a foundation of rootedness in Christ, living in and creating healthy community, it is here that we can co-labour with Christ, to paint on a solid canvas something that reflects beauty and creativity and that causes others to stop and see what is in front of them. And this is also the place where we get to dream.

To adventure.

To try.

While being deliberate to form a life which includes healthy rhythms and habits might help me find balance in my footing, there is a movement forward from this place that happens through a sense of calling that does not have to be "cookie cutter." It is not only for married people, just as it is not only for singles. And each one of us is invited into this process of stepping out into a life of passionate loving and service. This is not limited to the confines of a specific season of relationship. It is open to those who say: "I choose to embrace the gift I have been given, to content myself this season and to use this gift for the good of others and for God's glory."

And I dare say that the more we do, the more joy we experience, because we begin to live fully alive.

CHAPTER SEVEN

S. E. X.

I sat down to write this chapter and kind of froze. Truth is, I wrote the entire book and then came back to this chapter. Not because I did not want to write about it, but more because I was not sure if my thoughts on the subject were clear enough to write them out. I was not sure the right way to approach the subject, and maybe I just had more questions than answers. Questions that I am not sure I have answers to even now!

So often the topic of sex is avoided in Christian circles. We lightly brush past it in youth groups, assigning it to gender dichotomized life groups where the group leader is forced to incorporate it unplanned into Bible studies. At times it is cringe worthy.

But we do not actually engage with the topic in depth or in ways where open dialogue around the subject is encouraged. And we need to.

Sex is such an important part of our lives, whether we are married or not. We are created as sexual beings and we need to understand sex and our sexuality from a biblical perspective. Otherwise, our understanding will be formed around whatever narrative our cultures tell us is the best one. And these days, that is more than a little scary! The number of options we can choose from with regards to our gender identity, preferred sexual experiences, number of partners... it is all becoming more and more complex.

So, to simplify things, I am going to break down this chapter into three parts. *S, E,* and *X.*

S. Scrap the date.

E. Experience is everything.

X. /Y Chromosomes.

But I'm going to walk through them in reverse.

X/Y CHROMOSOMES

So let's start with X/Y chromosomes and perhaps science can help do the talking for me here.

We were created as sexual beings. This is biology. Male and female, as it says in scripture. Made with personalities, likes, dislikes and made in physical bodies which are sexual in nature.

As sexual beings, there will always be a question around how we handle our sexuality and our sexual desires. And the world will not make it easy for us. Everywhere we go, we are reminded of this. Sexually charged advertisements on buses, provocative commercials, scantily-clad storefront mannequins...

Sex sells because there is power in what sex can do to us. The appeal it has to us. The desires it arouses in us. Sex is powerful.

Genetically we were created to want sex. The ways in which our bodies respond to things we see or feel release hormones in our bodies that initiate a craving for sexual release. The endorphins that are released in our bodies while having sex were created to give us pleasure.

So, if all of this is chemistry and designed by God, is sex a bad thing? Absolutely not.

Scripture says that sex was God's idea, as Genesis 2:24 states: *"Therefore a man shall leave his father and his mother and hold fast to his wife, and they shall become one flesh."*

The physical makeup of a man and a woman compliment each other in ways no human could have invented. It is in the fibers of our being.

Sex is a good thing.

And if biology has not convinced you that sex is GOOD, Scripture reaffirms it again and again.

Genesis 2:25 speaks to Adam and Eve being naked in the garden together, unashamed.

Proverbs 5:18 speaks of the ways a husband is to delight in his wife's body: *"Let your fountain be blessed, and rejoice in the wife of your youth..."*

1 Corinthians 7:3-5 speaks to the duty of both husband and wife to please one another through sex, within the confines of their marriage.

God created sex to be a unifying act within the covenant of marriage which brought intimacy to union in a relationship. An act of cleaving to one another. An act that could (though not always) lead to procreation and a family line.

Sex was good.

But then entered sin and corruption. And suddenly what was good, even an act designed by God, was taken, and twisted into something that although good, was often pushed beyond what it was intended for.

It became a means to power. Abuse. Assertion. Addiction. Shame.

Sex was good, but it did not stop there.

And we so often don't either.

Our bodies are a temple for the living God.[1] And yet we have renamed, re-defined and re-aligned ourselves to things other than which God intended.

The way that we view and treat our sexuality so often disregards God's intentions for sex and cheapens it to a process of trial and error.

For singles who are not living in a marriage covenant, our culture has told us that we can still embrace sex as though it should be a part of our lives now. And so, we feed our sexual desires, either through casual hookups, relationships that do not last, or through the many virtual options available to us. Our generation treats sex as something at our convenience, asking: *"Why should singles have to suffer while married couples benefit from intimacy with one another? Surely God would not put unfair expectations on us when he was the one who created our bodies to experience and feel certain pleasurable things!"*

---

[1] 1 Corinthians 6:19.

But, just as Paul writes in 1 Corinthians 7:4 that husbands and wives do not have authority over their own bodies, those of us who are single are likewise committed to a relationship of purity which does mean abstinence from sex. Is this fair?

1 Corinthians 6:20 says that we were bought with a price. That we are called to glorify God in our bodies.

I was bought with a price. I have value. My body and my emotions have value.

This means accepting that I can be a sexual being, but I do not have to have sex. Simply because I do value who I am. And I value that I belong to God.

That sounds so simple. But it flies in the face of everything our culture tells us. That we can have it all. That if sex is good, then it is for everyone.

But this simply is not true.

Nor is it true that a person who lives a life without sex lives a life that is any less fulfilled than those that have it.

Jesus, just like many of his followers throughout time, never married and never had sex. This did not make him any less human, or less of an image bearer of God. Jesus, himself, shows us that a person is not defined by their sexuality or their sexual experiences. Like the Saviour we follow, we are defined by an identity that is so much deeper.

I can live a fully beautiful and rich life without ever having sex. Of course, I will wonder at what I am missing out on: I am only human. I will also have to learn how to handle my sexual desires because choosing not to have sex does not mean that I am no longer human and no longer deal with the wants of my flesh.

Paul speaks directly to these temptations in 1 Corinthians 7, stating these three things:

1. We will be tempted to sin sexually. It is a part of the human struggle. Paul writes *"because of the temptation to sexual immorality"*... as though it is a given.

2. We are able to exercise self-control over our bodies. Just because we have sexual desires does not mean we must act on them. Paul, in the next point, shows how marriage can provide a blessed place for those struggling with sexual desires to experience sex. (But this blessing of sex in marriage does not erase sexual temptation.) Having a spouse does not mean you will no longer be tempted sexually in other ways or by other people. Whether single or married, we are all called to walk in purity.

3. Paul shows here that *there are two possibilities*. Marriage or singleness. A life that includes sex and one that does not. Both are plausible. And in both cases, there are ways to live out these seasons of life in obedience to how God has called us to live with our sexuality and desires.

It might feel unfair that as singles we must deal with our biological sexual desires, to crave something that we cannot experience. We long for that type of intimacy with another, and yet we do not know if we will ever have the opportunity. But as satisfying as it might be to live in a covenant relationship and to enjoy the rights of a married couple, sex is not the answer to a craving for intimacy. If this were the case, we would see the instances of infidelity, pornography and lust disappear amongst people who have been 'happily married' for decades.

The temptations and sexual desires we have are a challenge for all people although, yes, there are unique ways that we, as singles must learn to navigate them. But we are all called to live in purity no matter the relationships we are invested in. And it is very possible to choose a life that honours God with how we treat our sexual desires, even if we never have sex.

E. EXPERIENCE

If covenant (as we will explore more below) says big picture, long term commitment, then experience says instant gratification, options, explore, and try out. Experience everything life has to offer, and sex happens to be one of those things.

We live in a time where experience is everything. In my home city of Vancouver BC, summer weekends amongst my friends are characterized by the experiences we have. Where did you hike? What pubs did you try out? How many kilometers did you drive or cycle? Sitting at home on a sunny long weekend while your friends are out exploring is almost considered a tragedy. Because what could you experience from staying around home? There is so much to see, and taste and smell and you'd better get out there while the sun is shining. We do have limited days of sun, after all. In many ways it boils down to "FOMO." *The Fear Of Missing Out*. So, if you are smart you don't.

I think at times we view sex and sexual experiences as something we are afraid to miss out on. If experience is everything, then why would we tell ourselves to wait? If there is something good to be tasted, it must be for now, and especially when our bodies are craving it. And there are so many ways to experience aspects of gratification for our sexual desires.

With many obstacles removed, we now have access to 'sex' in the privacy of our homes when no one else is in them. Lit up on computer screens, books, phones, or Netflix. The experience of sex has been brought close. Too close to say "No" to. And it is more than becoming a problem.

Gone are the days of one partner, or even a partner of the opposite sex. Experience tells us that we might like to try it all and with everyone. And somehow the sexual experiences we crave overrule the desire we have for purity. We want a quick fix for the cravings we have rather than looking deeper into the void we are trying to fill.

This leads us to a generation with pervasive problems of pornography, unsocialized youth, and abortions from unwanted pregnancies. It even leads to a disillusioned sense of self.

By believing that experience is everything, we are left in the chaos of our decisions. We have so many choices that we lose our freedom as we are drawn in an array of directions. We have given up on the belief that sex is a beautiful gift to be explored within a relationship of one man and one woman, and we have found ourselves stuck in a game where there are no boundaries, no end, and no way out.

Further, when we view sex as an experience we make it about ourselves, and what we get out of the deal. It is no longer a reflection of how we can serve one another. Sex, which from a biblical perspective was intended for marriage, is a place where a husband and wife model self-sacrificial love, just as Christ shows towards his bride, the church. Sex as an experience is all about me when I reject this mindset.

For those of us who trust the way of Jesus and the instruction in his word to us, we know that the gifts of God, even a good gift like sex, are to be treated in the way he designed them to be used. And the union which our physical bodies so long for cannot be experienced in quick fixes which only temporarily medicate the longings we have in our lives, whether stemming from our loneliness, disappointments, fears, or shame. Even a good desire for sex, can become something not blessed by God when used in ways it was not intended for.

I am 34 years old. I have wondered what sex is like. I have desired sex. But I am learning to trust God when he says that right now, this is not the best thing for me. It will not draw me closer to him and it will not lead to his blessing. But knowing this truth and walking in obedience is not always easy.

How can I protect my heart from the pull of temptations when they are so easily accessible, so pervasive? How can I trust in what I cannot see, when opportunities before me look pretty good right now?

Although I will not always understand the guidelines God gives us, as we walk in relationship with him we can trust that he is good. I can also trust in the experiences of others who have lived and learned in these areas of their lives. In chatting with married couples and older wise individuals, they have confidently shared with me aspects about their sexuality and their understanding of sex as people who have experienced it. I am encouraged by stories of perseverance through temptation, by the rewards of waiting for sex until the time was right, and by the healing God brought to wounds caused by sexual sin or abuse in their past.

God knew what he was doing when he gave us, his children, parameters around how we can value sex and why we need to also guard our hearts.

As singles it is easy to live out our sexuality in ways that no one knows. I will be honest, as a single person, people almost never ask me how I am doing with my sexual integrity. They have asked me how I was doing when I was dating, but not outside of that time frame. And while dating comes with its own set of temptations, we must as singles decide how we live with integrity before God in how we handle our sexuality on a regular basis.

It does not matter if you are male or female, 17 or 34.

For this reason, we need boundaries that will help keep us accountable. We all have coping mechanisms. Whether our struggle is with sexual desires, emotional desires, or other desires, without boundaries we so easily turn to numbing practices to medicate what we feel. If we just suppress our desires rather than work through them, this is often what happens. For some, this sort of medicating will be through pornography, masturbation or sexting while for others it will come through alcohol, Netflix, social media addictions, unhealthy dating habits, eating habits, work habits… things that will either help us forget the things we ache for, or that will keep us running after a sense of control of our lives.

Finding balance, and having boundaries in our lives, is not something that we can do alone. We need community. We need to ask ourselves who the healthy individuals in our lives are and have them walk with us. I mentioned earlier that community is so key in the boundaries we set in areas of our lives where no one sees. Finances. Time. Etc. When it comes to boundaries with sexual purity it can be hard to involve community in the struggles we have, because we feel ashamed. But whether it is around sexual addictions or poor habits, some of these practices can be really hard to kick on our own, and we need the strength of others. Shame would rather we keep hiding those addictions. After all, how could I tell anyone about this kind of struggle?

It has been a journey in my life to open up about my own areas of weakness. To invite community in. But the more I have allowed myself to be vulnerable with individuals whom I value, and whom I know have God's best intentions for me at the forefront of how they will counsel me, the more I have found safety in sharing and victory in healing in my own life. This requires work, vulnerability, consistency, and trust. But it is worth it.

I do not yet know if one day I will marry and have the experience of sex. I might, but I might not. And while the fear of missing out is pervasive in my generation, I recognize that fear is an emotion, and I refuse to be driven by what I feel.

I choose instead to trust.

SCRAP THE DATE

Finally, we have arrived at S.

Scrap the date.

I cannot tell you how many times I have now opened my phone to find a little email pop up with a Save the Date invitation. Yet another wedding this summer, another fun dance to look forward to with all my pals. I love dance parties and truly, if there was ever a time or place, weddings are it. Cram all your favorite people onto one tiny slippery space and watch them shed any inhibitions they normally wear, along with their shoes, blazers, and shawls - brilliant!

I remember as a youth having leaders in our youth group talk to us once about sex. They basically said: *"Wait. Save yourself for the day you get married. It will be worth it. Save the date."*

Their message was loud and clear, but there was not much of an explanation or framework around it. It was pretty much a win or fail situation. Those that made it to their wedding date still virgins were the winners. Everyone else had either lost or had a second-rate experience. And that was that. No space for questions.

Many of my friends growing up with this mentality got married quite young. Save the date, was all about the day they could have sex. It was what everything was building up to. I understood their excitement, obviously, but I also struggled to see that this was enough.

Youth group aside, the ideals of our classmates did not help. Because again, our culture was pushing us at younger and younger ages to believe that sex was the cool thing to do. It reinforced a misconstrued understanding putting the climax of relationship to an experience rather than a life of covenant.

But how do we live in a way where sex or even marriage (although good things) are not the goal but simply part of the bigger picture?

The biblical narrative is all about covenant. Now, my generation (yes you, millennials) cringe at the word covenant. It sounds old fashioned, outdated and constricting. A covenant is like a contract that you cannot get out of. And if ever there was something we hate: it is feeling that we do not have the freedom to leave. We want to have an out, always. How many parties have I tried to throw where friends were non-committal until the last minute, just in case something better came up? Then everyone decides to come, and I am short on cheese for my platter!

We are not good at sticking anything out. Our choices, our lifestyles, even our jobs… and our resumes reflect this. I should probably speak for myself, but I know I am not the only one in my age bracket whose resume contains such a wealth of experience. You would not be able to differentiate from my list of employment positions whether I am better qualified as a bus driver or a communications specialist. (On my Instagram account, I made both look pretty good.)

I broke into a cold sweat when signing a two-year cell phone plan a few months ago. What if I am no longer in the country then? Was it better to go with the pricier month-to-month no contract plan?

But despite sweating in the Telus shop, the older I get the more I do see that freedom actually begins with covenant. We need boundaries. We need commitment. And this is true for marriage and sex, but also with my relationship with God.

Covenant began with the calling of a people to live in right relationship with the creator of the universe who was jealous for their affections and who would not have them worship or give glory to another. His love was and still is true and faithful. It is inclusive of all people being invited into this right relationship with him, but it is exclusive of sharing this love with any other god.

And just as covenant is a key element of God's love story to us, so too, is the foundation of marriage not based upon a sexual experience but on a relationship of commitment. A relationship with boundaries which are not constrictive, but which lead to greater freedom to love another person. And it is within this covenantal space that sex may be enjoyed and celebrated.

Covenant says: *"I will wait."* It says: *"I will remain faithful. I am not in it for an experience, but for the long haul. For the relationship."*

Is this easier said than done? Absolutely.

The enemy will always attack what is precious to God. Sex symbolizes a joining of two people in a covenant relationship, a knowing of one another which is both intimate and designed by God for a good purpose. When our world, our sinful nature spurs us towards lifestyles that reject God's intended plan, we miss out on the greater things he has for us. We can also fall into cycles of shame, because deep down inside we know we were created for more.

As I have already stated, the desire for sex is not wrong. It points to the desire for intimacy that God put inside each one of us. To connect to others and to feel known. But ultimately our deepest desire is to know him. For those of us who are single, the longing for something we are not intended to have at this time in our life can only point us to the fulfillment that comes in knowing Christ. And should we choose to live outside this plan we will experience pain, even if not immediate, there will be consequences. Because we are choosing to love something more than we love the *one* who is jealous for us.

We only have to read the book of Hosea to see that this is not a new struggle. Hosea's relationship with his wife Gomer, a prostitute, is characterized by her unfaithfulness. It was a symbol of the unfaithful people of Israel to their God, Yahweh. In Hosea 2, we read about how Israel is an adulteress, bearing children out of wedlock, chasing after lovers. All her pursuits end in vain. She becomes lost, seeking after things that will always elude her, until she realizes she needs to return to her first husband, the one who provided for all her needs. The one who was faithful to her.

From the beginning we have walked away from covenantal relationship, muddling the waters with lust and affection for other things. We trade in purity for fleeting passion and somehow, we lose ourselves in the mix.

None of us are exempt from this. Our lusts, whether for sex or other things, can lead us down many roads which lure us away from the one we have been called to hold fast to. Our pride, our anger, our fear. We have all fallen short and the separation we feel between ourselves and God is deep. By choosing to live our lives in ways which satisfy our sexual desires now, we are sinning against God and walking in disobedience.

All of us have fallen short.

And thankfully, God knew this would be the case.

For the story does not end there.

In Hosea we read about the way Yahweh calls his people back to himself.

Hosea 14:1 says: *"Return, O Israel, to the Lord your God, for you have stumbled because of your iniquity."* Return to your maker. Come back to the one who has always loved you. Hosea 2:16-20 states: *"And in that day, declares the Lord, you will call me 'My Husband,' and no longer will you call me 'My Baal.' For I will remove the names of the Baals from her mouth, and they shall be remembered by name no more. And I will make for them a covenant on that day…*

And I will betroth you to me in faithfulness. And you shall know the Lord."

Our God is a God of redemption, and he has not changed.

No one has walked too far away from the love of God. No daughter or son's story is beyond redemption.

That was the reason I remember disliking the way my youth leaders talked about 'saving yourself for marriage.' Not because this was not a good thing, but because the way they framed it made it seem as though those who did not were disqualified from being used by God. They had ruined their stories.

Every single one of us is going to struggle with the affections of our hearts. For many, the most challenging area will be specifically related to our sexuality.

We have a God who calls us back to him, who redeems us, who washes us clean, and who points us again in the right direction, into relationship with him. Restored, renewed and covenantal. No longer characterized by shame, but by hope.

And he is so good to remind us that it is not about one date in time.

For those of us struggling with our sexual desires or the pulls of our hearts he is with us today, and he will still be with us tomorrow.

Our God is in it for the long haul.

CHAPTER EIGHT
i'm not single

People often guess I am about 10 years younger than I am. Partly this is because I look young, but I also blame it on having loads of energy and feeling no need to contain it. Life is too dull to become shells of the people we were meant to be! Thankfully experience and travel has shaped me to become quite malleable, and I have learned when to tone my exuberant self down just a notch to blend in when necessary. This has saved me on numerous occasions while travelling in relatively *quiet* communities

Most often the truth about my age comes out when conversation lends itself to discussion about work.

"International Development? Interesting. So where has your kind of work taken you?"

As country names begin to flow off my tongue, my conversation partners whom I have just met most often stop me mid sentence to ask: "Sorry, how old are you anyway?"

This is not a one-time occurrence. And embarrassingly enough, this has happened on several dates I have been on, uncovering the fact that I am significantly older than the men I find myself sitting across from in the cafe. I guess I can blame my sisters for that. Despite my being the youngest, my two brothers-in-law are one and five years younger than myself. I always thought I would get older brothers if my sisters ever married. I guess the joke was on me.

Well, the list of unique places I have worked not only gives away my age, but also speaks to the enriched experiences I have had working with a wide variety of teams. Many of my overseas teammates have differed greatly in age and background, be it economic, religious, or other.

And despite our differences in experience or worldview, there is one thing I have found pertinent to the health of any team I have been a part of. Not always by choice, but at times, more out of necessity, I have learned the importance that we see and act upon the premise that we are *all in*. The need to be fully invested, both in the team and in the work the team has been called to, is pertinent. Each person pulling their part. Each person seeing the value that the other brings.

It has made little difference which country I have worked in. The ability of my team to need and value one another in community is the starting point for everything good that happens. If we can work out the kinks in our own relationships, and find healthy ways to communicate, collaborate and value our differences, we will have a much stronger impact on the people we are there to serve.

It occurred to me quite suddenly, when I first moved overseas, that community was not optional. At least not optional if I wanted to thrive in the environment where I found myself. Moving across the world away from family, friends as well as the comforts and any semblance of home meant that the people I would work with needed to become that very source of support to me. Just as, I also quickly realized, I was to them. If I did not choose to invest in this community, I would be alone.

And let me tell you, I know from experience that is one of the hardest places to be.

I learned so much about the church when I worked overseas, because no matter where I went I found family. I found people who were in need, and I found people who were willing to embrace my needs. I found brothers and sisters who were willing to do life together, pursuing the call of God for us, living missionally where we were placed!

One of my favorite memories of working overseas was during my 2.5 years serving in Paris, France. The team I joined was working in a suburb assisting Arabic families, many of whom were immigrants and refugees to the city. It was a huge learning curve when I first moved to the not-so-French, Paris that I had heard much about. Not only was figuring out the mixed cultural norms and customs confusing, but the very streets in my neighbourhood were also bewildering. I got lost several times on the winding cobblestone corridors that circled around my apartment building. My home was the size of a cardboard box, and with a spindly little staircase leading to the fourth floor, visitors arrived huffing and puffing to my studio, cramming into my space for dinners, games nights and music theatrics.

Thankfully one of the families on my team was miraculously offered a house to live in with their three daughters. Downsizing from life on a farm in Kansas to city living was probably already enough of a shock for the family of five, so it was a relief that they were offered the space.

And they used their space so well.

Paul and Sara's home became my other home. I hung out with them and their kids several times a week. It felt so natural to do life with them. They had me over for dinners. I took their daughters on 'date-nights'. I played basketball with Paul and a bunch of friends on Monday nights. I went for prayer walks with Sara in the mornings. Although I had only just met my American friends, they felt like family within weeks. They would even let me use their home to host events as though I lived there. And they loved it. Or at least they made me feel like they did.

It was funny, but the more we invested in one another and learned how to support one another, the better we served the amazing families we were privileged to work with in our neighbourhood. Our love for one another was deep, and I truly believe this is why that love was able to spill out into the community around us. I cannot imagine what my time in Paris would have been like without Paul and Sara. They were my home away from home.

On several occasions after returning from overseas work trips which have varied in length of years to months, I have found myself struggling to see this sort of community in my hometown in Canada. Where are people like Paul and Sara? Perhaps we are just more comfortable with the way things are at home? Or we have coping mechanisms for doing life alone? Maybe we are just too busy? Or it could simply be that the intentionality of moving across the world to serve together demanded that we knew who we were serving with, and banked on the fact that we were *all in*. Dependant on one another, dependant on the vision that Jesus had for us, as a team.

I was reminded of a statement a friend shared with me after visiting a church in Vancouver a few years ago. He told me that he would never choose to attend that particular church because "they had no community to offer" him. I was puzzled by his comment, knowing that this friend talked about similar experiences in several other churches he had visited. Some churches were too small, others too big. Several of the churches he'd gone to had way too many seniors, and the people his age looked a little too hipster. People were not quite friendly enough, and it didn't look like their programs were all that interesting either.

It dawned on me that this friend was not talking about finding a real community, one that was created together. He was looking for a community that was already formed, and would meet his needs. As a single, he was looking for a church that would give him what he wanted. Friends his age, programs to suit his tastes. He wanted a church that would serve him well in his season of life.

As I later reflected again on his comment, I realized that this is the case for so many of us. We look for communities that will embrace us, cater to us, fill *our* needs. But this is not the truest sense of community. True community is one that emerges through lives that are shared. Lives that are poured out for one another. Through misunderstandings and reconciliation. Through imperfect attempts at loving and trying again. The reason I had felt such strong community in France was not because I walked into a perfectly formed group with the right number of singles my age. It was because we were committed to one another and the mess that we each brought. We struggled to love one another as we loved Jesus. Community was formed out of that place of loving and knowing one another intimately. And while as singles we hope to be a part of a church that lives in community in order to welcome others in, we have a part to play in where that community begins.

For most of us, community is not simply found. It is created. It is intentional.

Jesus has called us to live in community. We need each other. The church, *wherever we are*, is our team, it is our family. And in that family, we need to be all in, not only in our Sunday serving, but in the ways we invest in one another, in order to invest in the world. To do this we need to see and recognize the value that each of us bring to the church. The singles, the married people, the kids, the elderly. We need to embrace the needs that we see and share those that we bring.

If we fail to engage in these ways we hurt not only our own experiences, but we can deny an experience of community to others who could truly benefit from the gifts we bring, the encouragement we have to offer as a body.

We cannot operate as a body, as connected members with equally important functions, if we see ourselves as separate items of clothing, ones that can be put on and taken off when most convenient. We are fused together. Or at least we should be, in a most healthy sense.

Without a sense of connection, isolation can begin to eat away at our identity. We can also begin to believe definitions about ourselves that do not align with who we were created to be.

As singles we can find ourselves being defined by our relationship status.

Although most of us know that the term "single," simply means the state of being unmarried, we seem more inclined to steer our understanding of the word to the synonyms and connotations associated with this status.

Single = alone, not accompanied by another (or others), solo, by oneself etc.

I think, as singles, we need to ask ourselves: which definition are we believing?

The world may tell us that as singles we are living solitary lives. Ones that are uncommitted to any person (hence the freedom to engage in casual, destructive relationships, and habits). That we are (to use dictionary synonyms for single) odd, lone, solitary, individuals who are missing out on a fuller life of happiness. But nothing is further from the truth.

We choose how we define our singleness.

Have I, as a single, chosen to live my life in a way that separates me from a rootedness in community? Am I solo-ing through the hurdles of change, unaccompanied with my doubts and alone in my processing?

As one who professes faith in Jesus, I am not alone. *Firstly*, I am not alone, because I am found *in* Christ. My very being is founded within the life of a Triune community which fills me with presence, and a deep-rooted knowledge that I am accompanied, empowered, and loved by another. 70 times in the New Testament Paul writes that we are to be found *in Christ*. We are not apart from Christ, we are in him, just as his spirit dwells in us. When Emmanuel was announced to have come to Earth, the very idea that God was *with* us revolutionized how people were able to relate to God. How much even more so with the gift of the Holy Spirit dwelling inside of us! Darrell Johnson describes this communion with God in his book *Experiencing the Trinity*, as an invitation into the circle of God's "us-ness."[1] The Trinity, or the community of God, actually pulls us into an inner relatedness of that very community, or friendship. What an invitation it is to know and be known by the God of the universe. By the God who himself has always lived in relationship.

As a believer, I am not alone. Yes, I am single in relation to marital status, but not regarding my life as a person interconnected with God.

Neither am I alone if I engage with the gift of community that God has put around me, by engaging in the life of his church.

In Genesis 2:18, we read that God said of Adam: *"It is not good that the man should be alone; I will make him a helper fit for him."* Because Adam was created in the image of God, he is created in the image of the Trinity. It is for this reason, Darrell Johnson also writes that "lack or loss of relationship violates our essential nature, created to reflect the relational essence of God."[2] Our God is a God of community, and there is a reflection of this innate communion that his image bearers need in order to thrive. Man (Adam) was given instruction and purpose in his call to work in the garden, but there was a need for partnership. Adam needed a helper. He needed someone who would help him multiply the very essence of who he was created to be. And so God gives Adam a wife, Eve, and he was no longer alone. And

---

1   Johnson, Darrell. *Experiencing the Trinity.* Canadian Church Leaders Network. Print. 2021. pg 62.

2   Ibid. pg 53.

despite the fall of mankind and the decay of the world, Adam and Eve did multiply: through their offspring.

God gave Adam the privilege of a helper, one that worked alongside him.

As image bearers of God, singles share an internal desire for communion with others, to work alongside someone, to see a multiplication of their labour.

I do not believe that a spouse is the only answer to this cry for partnership, although it is one facet through which God can work. Otherwise, many of the singles we see named in Scripture would have needed to be married to accomplish the work of God through their lives.

But key to the impact of such individuals was a common way of living: in community where they did not function as lone agents. Even Jesus (who already had community in a Triune life) shared his life with his disciples. Paul (whom we believe was most likely single) ministered with several close companions as well as with the churches he ministered to, and who ministered to him. The fruit of their labour was not biological children but rather spiritual children. A family that grew because they worked together to proclaim the good news. Kingdom work. They did not see their lives or their mission as their own. It was to happen together. In community.

It is not good for man to be alone.

I am not single, in the way that I have often been defined as.

My life is anchored in community, in the body of Christ and in the life of a community who needs to know what a body really is. We are the body: imperfect men, women and children who are a family created with purpose. And in this family, I find people who truly know and love me. People who value my contributions, just as I value theirs. We do not always get this right, but we are trying. And the mess is beautiful.

But you must get close to see the beauty in the mess. You must 'un-alone' yourself to let people in. To walk together through the ups and downs and challenges of life. If I do not want to live a *single* life, by the definition that isolates, then I need to do my part, just as the church takes steps to include me.

As singles, we might say we want commitment: we want marriage, to commit to a person who will stick it out with us, even when they see the ugly sides of our personalities- the real us. But are we willing to commit to the church in the same way? Are we willing to get close enough to one another to see through the mess? This means our lives will mesh. And not just the singles with singles, but with all people.

I have never enjoyed communities that segregate by age. I attended a church once where most of the members were in their twenties and early thirties. I remember sitting in Bible study asking for advice about a big career change I was pondering. No one had any guidance to give me. Or at least no experience backing up the ideas they suggested, only speculation. I craved asking someone with more wisdom what they might have done in my situation. It was frustrating.

There is a place for children, youth, and young adults to gather in their specific demographics, yes. But this should always connect to the life of the church where all ages, all walks of life intersect. Because we are better for it. Families are not made up of teenagers, they are comprised of parents, grandparents, youth, and babies. If our families were all of one age, we certainly would find some households living on sugared cereal while others worked their lives away. There would be less learning and more comparing.

When we segregate by age or marital status, we begin to single people out for not being where others naturally find themselves in their age group. If I only hang out with friends in their mid thirties, I might be the only single one, and it tends to make me feel abnormal. We need to know and connect with people across different age categories and demographics. Older widows and younger singles find they have opportunities in common. When we mesh together, young families gain 'aunties' and 'uncles', youth gain mentors, widows gain friends etc.

So often, I hear singles say they have not found a place in the church. They feel crowded out by the growing number of young families. They feel used and a touch belittled when asked to serve in Sunday School, babysitting their peers' kids. It seems like they have been passed by in their life stage and serving others only highlights that fact. I hear married couples say that they miss being invited out by their single friends. For some, marriage meant they were no longer eligible to join in the Friday night games club or get asked to go skiing.

Perhaps if we were a little less segregated, and understood how much we each needed each other, this would not be the case.

Married life is not easy. Being a parent is not easy. It is a lot harder to criticize a young mom with two small children about how she has not been there for you when you do life with her and experience the lack of sleep and down-time she gets. It is a lot harder to critique a single man in your church for being distant when you have had him over for dinner and you hear the heart ache of nights alone, processing the breakup of a relationship he thought was heading towards marriage. As we learn to authentically do life together, we see that messy is a reality we all experience.

It does feel at times that there is a gap between the married people and those who are not. There are misunderstandings about how we are valued in the church. About how we can love and serve one another given our unique life stages. And I am not so sure we are good at asking how each other is doing.

We are all vital to the health and well being of the community. The closer we get to authentically forming this community, the less we feel the need to criticize or jealously point out the place of the other. Instead, we begin to honour and bless the roles that we each have in the seasons we might find ourselves in.

So how do we do this?

We have to make the choice to spend time together. In each others' homes. We need to learn to be more vulnerable about our lives, and invite one another in. We need to encourage one another to use our gifts and talents in the church rather than complain.

Singles can easily find other singles to surround themselves with. Someone to lament with in their shared season of life. We can pity ourselves, just as we sometimes receive pity from people in our communities.

And there are aspects of singleness that are really hard.

One of the greatest challenges I hear my single friends bemoan about is that so often they feel alone in the choices and plans they are making for their lives, when they wish they were making them with an invested partner. Someone who will ride out the implications of their choices with them. Where to live, which jobs to take, how to invest financially etc. I have to agree. It can feel lonely and difficult to navigate the future on our own.

It is easy, as singles, to see married couples and families and envy the instant community they have. We leave parties at the end of the night to debrief with... ourselves. We celebrate our victories and mourn our failures with friends, sure, but they are not with us the next morning when we wake up with an ache in our heart. Even more so, they do not have a shared understanding of the situation.

Simple things like vacationing can highlight the fact that we are single. Friend groups are constantly changing. People get married and are busy with married life.... But again, how we think about these things can easily lead us to operate out of a mindset of being in a place of lack, rather than living out of abundance.

But we need to break out of these unhealthy cycles.

I mentioned earlier that my teammates in France welcomed me into life with their family. I cannot begin to express what an impact this family had on me. Not just for the ways they loved me, but for the ways they consistently encouraged me in knowing my place and in using my gifts as a single in the ministry we were a part of. They never pitied my marital status but rather supported me to use it!

I remember one day Sara and I went for dinner downtown, leaving Paul with the kids. It was fun for her to go out without carrying extra backpacks and sleepy children. It was fun for me to talk to someone my age who cared about the same things I did. While stuffing our faces with Italian pasta (in Paris, I know), Sara said that she wanted to thank me for being a single. She had been thinking about the way my singleness was a gift to our team, allowing me to serve in a unique way to the people around us.

I had never had someone thank me for being single before. It struck a deep chord within me.

Sara's honoring of my life stage was beautiful. I had always felt so much appreciation for the kind of mom Sara was. She was patient, generous of her time and was always listening. I loved how having kids opened doors for her to connect with other moms. How she boldly walked through those open doors, despite being a little shy and not having all the language or knowing all the cultural norms yet. I love how we both missed family and found sisters in each other. We were able to pray for one another, we laughed all the time, worked out together, and even cut each other's hair. If there was anyone who was living the world's most beautiful life, I thought it was her. And yet, she wanted to tell me that she thought my life stage was beautiful and a gift to her and to our community.

I believed it when Sara said this. But I also needed to believe it myself, rather than focusing on the things that were hard. To recognize that my singleness not only came with challenges but with many blessings.

Community can either HELP or HINDER me in recognizing the gift of singleness that I have been entrusted with. And it is difficult when we feel, as singles, that we must fight for that recognition that singles do have a voice, a place to serve when we might already be struggling to believe it ourselves.

We so need each other.

We need to learn to speak value over one another, without trying to rush one another into the next stage of life.

It is funny to me how we so often try to change the status of a single person. *"If only that single person could be married..."* When married couples struggle through challenges, we encourage them as a husband or wife to learn how to be the best spouse they can be, even when it is not easy. Now while we may not have committed our lives to singleness (like those in marriages), as singles we are called to pursue what God has for us in each period of our lives, and therefore we should aspire to be the healthiest follower of Jesus we can be.

We do not need to change people to be more like we are, we need to empower people to be more like Jesus.

What if the questions I was most often asked was not about whether I wanted to get married or if I had met any cool guys lately, but rather, "How is the Spirit leading you in this time of life"? "Where is he calling you to have an impact in your workplace and in your friend circles as you let him shine through you?" And what if we began asking each other "How can the church come around you in those areas to both equip you and pray for you?" "Where do you feel led to use your gifts, your voice, your passion?"

There is SO much good that our singleness brings to the body of Christ!

Could we learn to celebrate who each other is without having to tie that into a future projection of where that person needs to be?

I wonder though if, in our churches, we fail to have a vision for singles because we consistently return to projecting the path towards marriage. We need to stop telling singles that singleness is just a time of preparation for marriage. Can we instead, come alongside those who are struggling to find their purpose and help them discover their gifts? What about finding places for them to serve and give? Let's make space for singles in leadership positions, letting them use their voice, their extra time and their capacity. I think we would be amazed if we did this, how singles would step up to lead, to risk and to inspire others to do the same. We need to share that vision and not constantly cut it off by assuming the single life will end, because that is not a guarantee.

The more authentically we live as a team made of many unique body parts, the more we realize we each have our areas of gifting, just as we have our areas of pain, and it makes us a little more appreciative of who each other *is*, and less competitive of where we are different.

I am a part of a bigger body, one that hurts, celebrates, corrects one another, and takes ground for the Kingdom, together.

Just as being a team includes doing life together while valuing the contributions of each person in the community, there is also a need to embrace the mission of the body.

We have such an incredible calling as the church to be the hands and feet of Christ in a world that is aching to be loved, to be included, to be invited. We are all called to let our lights shine. Truly, they will know us by our love. The extent to which we know and love one another will draw many to want to know the love of Christ. It will compel others to know what it is that motivates and transforms us to be more Christ-like. We should be a safe place where anyone feels welcomed. A place where there is opportunity for the gospel to be lived out and clarified through words as well as deeds.

We are not perfect, and we will not live out our calling perfectly, but in the body we have the perfect place to practice. To forgive and reconcile. To extend grace to one another. In our church family, we have one of the best places for community to practice what it looks like to embrace the journey of people who are not alike, and who might never share the same pursuits outside of this mission. We can start by loving one another in our different journeys through life. And we can learn, in humility, how to relate to those who are walking on very different paths than we might ever find ourselves.

As people who are called to ONE mission, but who are beautifully diverse in the ways we were made, we are a reflection to the world of a creator God. We are the place where unity of purpose trumps our differences and dislikes. Where our differences are celebrated, and the uniqueness of our strengths brings richness to our community and our experiences regardless of race, background, or marital status. This is what will show a world in need the power of the gospel at work in a group of very flawed human beings.

And while it is nice to talk about this, I want to point out a few practical ways we can actually take steps towards this.

The more time I have spent with my married friends, the more I have realized there are opportunities for me to bless them and learn from them. I have learned the importance of continuing to invite my married friends to join in the activities I am doing. For friends with children, there are times where I can bless them by going to them, bringing adult conversation to a day of toddler feedings and bath times. Sometimes I can offer to stay with their kids so they can have a long-awaited date night. I can pray for my friends' marriages with them and ask how they are doing in this regard. The opportunities are endless, and the list could grow to include the youth around me, the elderly, the children. There are so many beautiful ways we, as singles, can invest in the lives of others in our community.

Likewise, there are many practical ways I believe our community can learn to love on singles. Sometimes the needs we have are not as pronounced. We do not have diapers and marriage struggles, but we have our own challenges that we are working through.

I thought I would share a few of the opportunities that came to mind. Ways that the church can practically encourage singles.

1. Invite singles into your family. Let them experience the highs and lows with you. The adventures and the hard days of being a parent. Be willing to take time to leave your kids with your spouse once in a while to go see your single friend too. It shows them that you value them and you don't always expect them to come to you.

2. Avoid telling singles what they already know. "You're getting closer to the end of childbearing years." No single woman ever needs to be told that. And yet, this past month, I was told this two times. First of all, I am 34. I'm pretty sure I'm not past childbearing years. Secondly, not being a mom is one of the biggest losses many women nearing the end of their 30's think about. Highlighting the loss of a dream might not be the best encouragement.

3. Include singles in pre- and post-event happenings. Sometimes as singles, it is hard to always go to events alone. Especially if the event you are going to includes mostly or all married couples. Offer to drive together. Debrief funny moments of the night with them on the ride home.

4. Engage with singles in ways that don't always make them feel like the odd ones out. Dinner parties can feel so awkward when you are the only single. Try discussing topics that include everyone and which do not single out the unmarried persons around the table. Be okay to not sit with your husband or wife for one meal. Switch up places around the table so the single person is not at the end by themselves every time they go to a dinner party.

5. Look for ways to celebrate with singles. They may not be having engagement parties, weddings, baby showers and baby birthdays every few months, but they do have other significant things happening in their life. Champion their successes, not just their birthdays which every human being is entitled to. Find a reason to celebrate their life stage with them.

6. Never pity a single. Have compassion on their struggles, yes. At times, we really do need this. But, if you truly value a single and understand the amazing calling singles have been given, you will not pity them. That they have much to contribute to the body of Christ. You will help them recognize, even when they doubt or struggle to see their own value, that they are fully embraced and loved as they are. Also, don't look down on singles as though they are missing out (or that they belong on a junior varsity team). Married couples and

parents are missing out on other things. Both have benefits and challenges.

7. Process hard decisions with singles. Often singles can feel very alone in the choices they have to make. There is a longing to have an invested partner who makes those decisions with them. Take time to hear out your single friends and listen to their struggles. Pray with them rather than offering quick advice.

8. Ask open ended questions. Questions that do not assume a single feels a certain way about their singleness. "How are you doing?", can suffice.

Remember that everyone is unique. No one single will have the same journey as another, so we need to stop projecting onto singles how they should or should not be feeling, or insinuate as much by our questions.

Some of my married friends have told me that their first year of marriage was incredibly difficult. Others felt it was so full of joy they could not believe how easy it was. Our relationships cannot be compared, but we do need to learn to care for one another in the times where our relationship status seems to reflect our desires, and the times when it feels wanting.

As a single, I need the community God has given me to challenge me and encourage me in various aspects of my life. There have been times where this has been challenging for me. Where I have felt that there is no space for me as a single. Where I do not know where to invest my gifts and my passion. I have also experienced rich church community that has welcomed me in my life stage as an integral member in the life of the church. And in these spaces it has been more than rewarding to participate.

These are the places where I have felt safe to bring my seeking friends, because I know that my community will love them well.

Scripture points to a way of life that is beautiful. One that is lived in pursuit of Jesus, in community, for the world. Each of us, whether single, married, in a relationship or grieving a relationship is going to face challenges in how we walk through life. But we do not have to face these experiences alone.

We do not face our battles alone.

We do not win our victories alone.

I was reminded this week of Exodus 17:8-13. The passage talks about a time when the Israelites were struggling to follow God through the desert. Tired, exhausted, and learning to trust, they came into a battle with Amalek. Moses, having sent out Joshua and some of his men to fight for Israel, stood at the top of a hill overlooking the battle. He held the staff of God in his hand, knowing who he was trusting to fight this battle. As the battle raged on, Moses saw God bring victory for the Israelites, so long as the staff of God in his hands was held high. When Moses' arms grew weary, the battle would turn. Fatigued, after hours on the hill, Moses could not maintain his posture. Not without the help of his friends Aaron and Hur, who stood beside Moses. They did not take the burden of lifting the staff from Moses, but rather helped raise his arms. And in doing so, they saw victory, as the Lord defeated their enemy before their eyes right until the sun set.

We are not called to fight our battles alone. We are not called to walk through life without the support and love of the people God has put around us. And I hope that in the church we can lift one another's hands, carrying whatever he has given us to him, watching while he brings victory.

If, as a single, I can learn to be vulnerable with my community, about where I need support, I might create opportunities for friends to stand with me.

I need to be honest about the things people do that are helpful, and when beneficial, communicate those that are hurtful. If we hide from one another the places where we hurt, we also rob each other of the ability to show up for one another. Vulnerability is not an easy thing, but it changes our relationships and allows us to see into each other's worlds. We need each other invested, close up, in our messy, messy worlds.

I am not single. Not in the ways the world defines singleness.

I may not have a husband right now and while at times this can be a challenge, I have a wealth of brothers, sisters, nieces, and nephews, biological and other. I have spiritual babies that the Lord has entrusted me to journey through this season with and I have spiritual parents that are helping to guide me.

I have been entrusted with a beautiful life. One that is full of surprises and unknowns in which I am called to follow. Not the narrative of my culture but a path that is centered on Christ. I am called to dream and to embrace the adventure that I am already on. In my singleness I have a place to use my gifts, to embrace a calling to love others. I have a community where I can practice using these gifts and share them with the world through creative ways, rejecting a posture of consuming or whatever message my culture throws at me.

As someone who is not married, I am not lacking. I am complete and completely loved.

So when people tell me *"When you get married…"*, I can only shrug.

Because the way I am choosing to live my life right now, wholeheartedly embracing the path I have been given, is the answer to my very own question: *"And if I don't?"*

Other titles from **Schleitheim Press**:

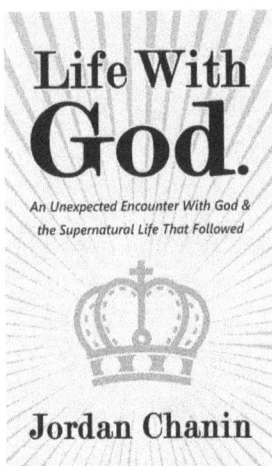

Life with God: An Unexpected Encounter with God and the Supernatural Life that Followed

By Jordan Chanin

ISBN: 978-1-990389-03-0

Growing up without faith, Jordan Chanin's life was a pursuit of partying, sex and the next drug high. After an encounter with God during the throes of a family tragedy, he underwent a radical life transformation. In this original, biographical publication by Schleitheim Press, witness the miraculous impact that comes from devoted Christian life. Through this book be inspired to begin your own supernatural journey with God.

The Fateful Years: A Mennonite in Russia, 1913-1923

By Gerhard Lohrenz

ISBN: 978-1-990389-01-6

What was it like for the Mennonite community during the social and political upheaval in Russia during 1913-1923? This work of fiction, in print for the first time in 40 years, blends both personal experience from the author and stories from other first-hand accounts. Gerharld Lohrenz (1899-1986) was a leader in the Manitoban Mennonite community, serving as Principal of the Mennonite Brethren Collegiate Institue and later pastoring the Sargent Avenue Mennonite Church.

Learn more at **SchleitheimPress.com**

CPSIA information can be obtained
at www.ICGtesting.com
Printed in the USA
LVHW051004250623
750723LV00009B/555